PRAISE FOR
ONAL TRANSITIONS

"Whether you've become shipwrecked on the shores of your old life, sit with dreams of better times, or simply feel the rumblings of change deep inside, *Personal Transitions* is a powerful spiritual compass. It will bring comfort to the confused, perspective to the perplexed, and a sense of excitement to the exhausted."

— *SARAH ROZENTHULER*, chartered psychologist, leadership development consultant, and author of *Life-Changing Conversations*

"Steve Nobel offers an elegant and wise exploration of the nature of life's most challenging and rewarding times: those that call us to change direction and open to something completely new. Such times call us to deepen our relationship to ourselves as well as to something greater. Amidst the increasingly changing times we live in, this book is a timely guidepost to awaken our innate wisdom and find a passage to greater fulfilment."

— *AMODA MAA JEEVAN*, spiritual teacher and author of *How to Find God in Everything*

"*Personal Transitions* is a vitally important book for our time. Steve weaves spiritual, psychological, and metaphorical concepts to bring us into a higher understanding of what on earth is going on right now. He outlines the journey of personal transition and puts it into a larger planetary context. He works with a truly multi-layered (dimensional) approach, and wonderfully maps the way to know our inner radiance. So if you want to awaken the limitless potential within you and emerge into the true brilliance of your own light this is the book for you."

— *VAZ SRIHARAN*, founder/director of The London College of Spirituality.

"There are few subjects more important than how to navigate the big transitions in life. A transition is more than a change; it is a crossing over from one state to another. It can amount to dying and coming back. Steve Nobel offers us wise and very human guidance on how to release what is holding us back, recover our inner compass, and manifest our dreams of a richer and juicier life. He is a teacher who walks his talk, and is not shy about sharing his own experiences of falling down and sometimes struggling to get up again. This is the best kind of teacher, and *Personal Transitions* will help you to find and follow your own path of heart, the only path worth following."

— *ROBERT MOSS*, author of *Conscious Dreaming* and *Dreaming the Soul Back Home*

"This book came to me at a time when I was undergoing major changes in my life. These changes were no mere picnic in the park, but vast shifts that were affecting me on a deep level. I was certainly questioning everything—from my career to my relationships and even, heaven forbid, my spirituality. *Personal Transitions* is a powerful read: it helps you understand, accept, cope, and surrender to whatever kind of transition you are going through. The end game of this book is to help you step into your light and shine."

— *ALEXANDRA WENMAN*, editor of Prediction Magazine

"We humans are habitual creatures; we do not like sudden or fast paced change because it takes us deeper into the great unknown. If you are in a period of radical change then Steve Nobel's *Personal Transitions* will take you firmly by the hand, give you the structure and tools to step forward in your life, and ultimately assist you to wake up. A must read! "

— *NICOLAS DAVID NGAN*, author of *Your Soul Contract Decoded: Discovering the Spiritual Map of Your Life with Numerology*

"Steve Nobel dives into the painful but transformative subject of transitions, exploring individual and global change. *Personal Transitions* offers guidance to help you navigate your own life changes (whether you've chosen them or not) as gracefully as possible. While recognizing that all transitions are different, Nobel considers how much more frequent a part of life such soul-shakers have become. After all, when we've come through a transition, there is gratitude for the better life the chaos and pain ultimately cleared the way for. A book that inspires a real sense of hope."

— *EVE MENENDES CUNNINGHAM*, freelance psychology, health, and well-being journalist/writer, owner at the Feel Better Every Day Consultancy

"Transitions are the exciting, scary, and potent moments in our lives that reveal our true soul potential. *Personal Transitions* navigates you gracefully through the abyss and ascendancy of significant life moments. Always insightful, wise, and inspirational, Steve Nobel shares how transitions are a required part of human existence and how they have the power to propel us individually and collectively to our greatest and highest purpose."

> — *CLARE RUSSELL*, intuitive expert, founder of Metalife and Sacred Destinations

"Steve Nobel has written an important and engaging book, full of compassion, insight, and practical tips to help us understand and more gracefully navigate our transitions. I started reading his book on a grey-sky day when feeling somewhat downhearted about my own current transition. Four chapters in, I was feeling full of optimistic excitement about what I've already achieved and all the marvellous opportunities ahead."

> — *NEIL DEL STROTHER*, author, freelance journalist, and Journey Practitioner

"This is a valuable and heart-felt book, written with much knowledge and generosity. The author has clearly experienced a powerful life transition and reflected on the experience very deeply, studied the anatomy of transition, and drawn much learning from it to share with others. As he suggests, in these turbulent times, we all need the find the courage and willingness to understand and fully embrace transition, so we can free ourselves from the collective grip of outdated and damaging patterns. This book can help us do that."

> — *JUSTINE HUXLEY*, Director of St. Ethelbergas Centre for Reconciliation and Peace

"Whether change is chosen or thrust upon us, welcome or unexpected, *Personal Transitions* charts our transformative journey and guides us from caterpillar through cocoon to butterfly. This book is about true transformation and helps you get the best outcomes from the changes in life."

> — *CLAIRE EDWARDS*, Cygnus Review

"As we go through transition globally more and more of us are experiencing it personally. This book will help you to cope with it, even embrace it. It will help you to move home, metaphorically, when you need to rather than, as Steve Nobel puts it, simply moving the furniture of your life around.

— *CATHERINE G. LUCAS*, author of *In Case of Spiritual Emergency*

"Steve Nobel is an explorer of the soul and this is a valiant and honest exploration of the mystical, psychological and subconscious realms. His work is a valuable addition towards an essential journey for humanity."

— *MALCOLM STERN* - co-founder of Alternatives, psychotherapist and co-presenter of Channel 4s *"Made for each other"*.

"Steve is a very special spirit who understands both the personal challenges that people face in life and work – and the path of self discovery that resides below. Through his books, talks and life's work he helps people seamlessly explore and discover in a way that is apt for that individual / soul. That is a remarkable skill to have. His knowledge of the spiritual landscape is remarkable his personable friendly style is the mark of his authenticity. Keep up the fantastic, noble work."

— *RASHEED OGUNLARU,* Business coach, motivational speaker, and author of *Soul Trading*

PERSONAL TRANSITIONS

Beyond the Comfortable into the Real

Steve Ahnael Nobel

FINDHORN PRESS

© Steve Ahnael Nobel, 2014

The right of Steve Ahnael Nobel to be identified as
the author of this work has been asserted by him in accordance
with the Copyright, Designs and Patents Act 1998.

Published in 2014 by Findhorn Press, Scotland

ISBN 978-1-84409-651-0

A CIP record for this title is available from the British Library.

Edited by Nicky Leach
Front cover photograph by Bo Hansen
Cover design by Richard Crookes
Interior design by Damian Keenan
Printed & bound in the EU

Published by

Findhorn Press

117-121 High Street,

Forres IV36 1AB,

Scotland, UK

t +44 (0)1309 690582

f +44 (0)131 777 2711

e info@findhornpress.com

www.findhornpress.com

Contents

Acknowledgements

I want to thank all friends and family for humouring and supporting me in my journey these past few years. Big love to my little spiritual community in East London and all the gorgeous peeps, past and present, I have sat and had tea with there.

Thank you to all the amazing spiritual teachers I have heard, read, met, or trained with over the past 20 years.

Thank you, Alternatives, for being such a bright communal light in the centre of London. Your light drew me in so many years ago. I am honoured to have served you for 13 inspiring years as a director. I have met many wonderful souls there and I will always remember the great 'Mother Ship' fondly in my heart.

Special thanks to the late Gill Edwards, who woke me up many years ago; the great mythologist Joseph Campbell, whose wisdom inspires me so; William Bridges, for his brilliant pioneering work into the area of transitions; and David Whyte, whose courageous poetry and conversations upon the many frontiers we each face in our lives has proved so useful in my own journey.

Thank you, Ursula, for all the love you shared with me for many years. Bless you, Lisa, for the time we spent together, and for revealing my soul journey.

Thank you, Emma, for your compassionate support in our weekly transpersonal therapy meetings. You witnessed so much of my inner turmoil.

Much love to my children, Lynda and Peter, and to my granddaughters, Eva and Isabella, (who were both born during my recent transition).

Finally, I dedicate this book to all the folks out there who are going through a transition right now. Please know that you are all part of the essential 'Great Work' of awakening happening across the planet right now.

Introduction

All around us in nature, life unfolds
according to certain inner designs.
A rosebud opens into a rose, an acorn grows into an oak,
and a caterpillar emerges as a butterfly from its cocoon.
Is it unreasonable to assume that human beings
share this quality with the rest of creation—
that, we too, unfold according to an inner plan?
— *HOWARD SASPORTAS*

This book is about a powerful and unique process that happens at important moments in our lives. This process I call 'personal transition,' although it is happening at a personal and also global level right now. At a personal level, it is about radical inner and outer transformation. At a global level, the planet is going through a major shift right now. This is a shift in consciousness that will take some decades to complete.

Personal transitions are at the heart of this global shift, because they are a primary way that the soul gets us to wake up to the reality of the essential self and to the delusions of this world. Because of this, a transition is not something our personality or ego-mind welcomes. We are conditioned to seek comfort, pleasure, and the familiar; yet, so long as we are alive on the earth, we are subject to evolutionary and spiritual forces that want us to open, grow, deepen, and awaken.

Change, of itself, does not necessarily lead to personal growth or awakening. Change is two-dimensional, whereas a transition is three-dimensional. Change is like moving along from point A to B: there is no depth, merely movement. A transition involves depth, because our heart and soul are engaged. A change is purely external—you can change your brand of toothpaste, your girlfriend/boyfriend, your home, friends, relationship, or career and still remain practically the same on the inside. A transition, on the other hand, alters our psychology—the way we think, the way we feel and how we perceive the world. Transitions force us to address the important questions of existence: Why are we here? What do we want to do? What direction do we take? Where in the world do we truly belong? These run counter to other more superficial questions, such as: How can I get more of what I want? How can I make more money? How can I climb the status ladder faster?

A transition alters our core beliefs, which affect the choices we make; change may alter our outer circumstances, without liberating us in any way. Transition is a liberating force that helps to make our lives ultimately lighter and easier. Change can happen without affecting the general direction of our lives; a transition alters our course and changes our future destinations. Change is purely material, whereas a transition impacts our consciousness and spiritual awareness. Sometimes a transition takes us soaring up to the light; or it can take us into the soil of our being, where we face old shadows that need to be witnessed and integrated in our experience. A transition is powerful but does not always feel convenient. A transition disturbs our routine, shakes us up big time, and edges us out of our familiarity zones.

There is so much to say about the process of transition, and one book may not be enough. That being said, it is important to add the following, before diving into the book itself:

- The transition process helps us release an outdated phase of life and embrace a new one. Every transition has five phases: Soul Tension, Choice-Crisis, Release, Recalibration, and Renewal.
- A transition changes us from the inside out—we are no longer the same person on the other side. A shift can happen on many levels at once: physical, mental, emotional, and spiritual.
- No two transitions are the same in content, although all have the same structure and progress in the same way. The process is not haphazard or random, even if it appears to be;
- All transitions are big, but some are bigger than others. A big transition strips us down to the core, changes our outer life, then rebuilds us from the inside out. Such a major journey we may take just once or at most a few times in our life.

Who Is This Book For?

This book is written for anyone who feels that they are entering a period of transition. You might already be part way through the journey and want some advice on what to expect and what to avoid. Perhaps you are feeling a little stuck in your journey and want to know how to move on in the process. Perhaps a loved one is going through a transition and you want to find out more about the process so that you can gently advise or nudge them in the right direction.

This book is offered as a practical guide, with information and advice on navigating each stage of the journey. It is not offered as any kind of dogmatic truth on the subject. It is written to help you navigate an important journey.

There are all kinds of transitions—from life shifts, such as adolescence to adulthood and midlife, to smooth transitions, where we follow a meaningful dream into a new phase of life, to the more difficult transitions, which involve some form of life or existential crisis. Some transitions include some aspect of spiritual awakening that can feel confusing or scary. With that in mind, this book offers information on topics such as: spiritual emergence, spiritual emergency, kundalini awakening, shamanic illness, dark night of the soul, ayahuasca, and much more. On a final note, I would say if you are drawn to this book, then your inner self must in some way have led you to it for some reason you may soon discover.

An Overview of the Transition Experience

Transitions can be smooth, joyful, and graceful; alternatively, they can be rough, confusing, and painful. There are also super-rough transitions, which often offer the greatest gifts of all. To sum it all up, a transition can help us:

- Embrace soul tension and soul calling;
- Strip away the unreal and the superfluous;
- Let go of limiting conditioning and identity;
- Heal old emotional wounds;
- Embrace our deep vulnerability;
- Handle ambiguity, challenge, and uncertainty;
- Transform old limiting habitual patterns
- Edge us out of our familiarity/safety zones;
- Stretch, grow, mature, open, and awaken;
- Develop a strong stable core;
- Become more adaptable, capable, and resilient;
- Reach new levels of authenticity and integrity;
- Experience a deepening of surrender and trust;
- Release the fullness of our inner potential;

- Get clear on true purpose and direction;
- Find a true sense of belonging and home in the world;
- Restructure the ego into a strong vehicle for our inner light;
- Activate and sharpen our intuition and inner knowing;
- Expand and strengthen the connection to our Higher Self;
- Allow in more flow, grace, and synchronicity;
- Contribute meaningfully to the great global awakening.

My Own Transition Experience

The idea for this book came in 2010, when a big transition unexpectedly erupted in my life. This was not my first transition, although it was the most challenging. Putting aside my birth, a difficult adolescence, and a painful entry into the world of work, my first big transition came in the mid-1980s. I was working in a career I disliked intensely, and I was married with one daughter and a son on the way. Then I hit a crisis and could not stand my life anymore. So after some painful reflection, I made preparations to press the eject button on my life.

I planned it down to the last details, and as I was losing consciousness, I heard a voice speak inside my head, saying, *There is hope!* This voice was like nothing I had heard before—there was something in the voice that conveyed certainty and authority. So I aborted my little escapade and was soon carted off to Accident and Emergency at the local hospital. The next morning, I awoke to several relatives from my wife's side of the family gathered around the bed. It was one of those moments of intense embarrassment and relief. I took a year off work and then resigned from my job. I went into long-term therapy for several years, and soon after began a new career in local government.

The next transition came a few years later, in 1993, when my marriage of 15 years ended. This was both a painful time and one when I found myself in a vortex of rapid change. In rapid succession, I met many spiritual healers, teachers, and new friends and started training in all kinds of weird, wacky, and wonderful things. I was meditating for hours every day, leaving the 'normal' world behind and opening to a new space of greater internal light and possibility.

The next transition came a few years later, when I left my second career in local government after 10 years. I felt an inner calling to align my career with my spiritual life, but I had no idea how to do that. Finally, one day I asked the Universe out loud, 'Should I resign from my job?' I waited, and within 48 hours I received a clear set of signs in response, so I resigned the next day. After a bumpy patch of a year or so, a happy set of synchronicities led me into a new career and also a wonderful new romantic partnership. I settled down into a regular rhythm, believing I had done my fair share of transitions and that my life was basically sorted. How wrong I was! When the most recent big transition hit, it led me into a dark, volatile, and profound period of my life.

Writing and Researching This Book

The research and writing of this book took me slightly over three years to complete. During this time, I was often asked what I was up to. After I explained, the most common response went something like, 'Oh, yeah, everyone is going through that right now!' Needless to say I took this to be an encouraging sign that I was on the right track.

This book has been written in real time, meaning I was writing it as I was going through my transition. This book, therefore, could only be complete when my own transition process was completed. It is written in two parts. The first part, Of Soul and Gravity, puts the transition process into context. Here, we explore the important questions of soul and gravity, as well as the different types of transition. The second part, The Timeless Way of Transition, deals with the actual process or experience of transition. In this part, I share more of my own recent super-rough transition.

I would say this has been the toughest and most transformational period of my life to date. This book was completed over Easter 2014, when a powerful Cardinal Grand Cross astrological alignment occurred, with an exact hit on my natal Libra sun. Easter and the Grand Cross both connect to the energies of crucifixion and resurrection, which seemed a perfect metaphor describing my own transition journey and a good place to finish.

Warm wishes
Steve Ahnael Nobel
April 2014

PART ONE

Of Soul and Gravity

1

A Question of Soul

*Our soul, our true self, is the most mysterious, essential,
and magical dimension of our being. In fact, it is not a separate
reality, as traditional Western thought views it, but the cohesive
force that unites our body, heart, and mind. It is not a ghost
trapped somehow in the physical machinery of our body
but the very essence of our being.*

— *GABRIELLE ROTH*

A transition is a life-altering event, and although the content will differ from person to person, the context is generally the same. A transition comes to shake up our lives, open and move us, and shift who we are being and becoming in the world. It comes to help us, reconnect us to a sense of wholeheartedness, return us to a state of resourcefulness, and redirect us to a whole new track or orientation in life.

As perhaps you can appreciate, a transition is a major experience that leaves us transformed, both inside and out. Transitions are not random events; they are orchestrated by a deeper intelligence to disrupt and also liberate our lives. We could call this deep intelligence by several names: Life Force, Soul, Higher Self, Tao, Buddha Nature, and Christ Consciousness. There are many names, but when it comes down to it, the name does not matter; the important thing to remember is that we are more than this body, this personality, this collection of ego selves, this social identity. Soul operates on many planes of existence, and Earth is but one. It is as Master Jesus said, "In my Father's House there are many rooms" (John 14:2).

Not all planes are as dense or as challenging as this one. Beyond this plane, the laws of time operate differently. Here, time is linear, but in the realm of soul, past, present, and future are not so distinct. This is how soul can create synchronicities, which are events in the coming future. Soul can also set up current events to heal past karma. Soul is more powerful than we realize.

In this world, soul is mostly misunderstood or goes unrecognized. When we come out of the birth canal, we forget we are light and start to live under the illusion that the body is all there is. This then leads to the idea that without the physical body there would be no consciousness, no existence. This is not the case. We are sleepwalkers in this world, and a transition is there to remind us that our personality and body are not the centre of the universe. The body is impermanent, and one day its strength and beauty will pass away.

A transition comes to wake us up from our illusions and delusions. If we are worshipping false idols, then we are not honouring the light within. A transition is meant to open us to the realm of soul. A transition helps us experientially cultivate authenticity, a resilient spirit, a guiding sense of trust and faith, and a meaningful engagement with life. A transition reminds us that life is no mere set of routines. The soul is eternal, and it incarnates here on Earth to learn, celebrate, stretch, and grow. If we forget this, we lose our ability to smile, laugh, and cry.

Life can be hard, and most of us are taught to toughen up, hide our vulnerability, and get real. Our peers support us in achieving, chasing, and competing, or on the flip side, getting our needs met by shouting the loudest or playing painful victim games. We become used to putting on a brave face or trying to look good or maintain our cool. This begins in childhood and kicks off in earnest during teenage years, when we are scrambling to find a new sense of acceptable identity in the world. (Adolescence is itself a major time of transition, which sets the scene for our adult years.)

Transition was once mainly a simple yet profound process of maturation. Living in the modern world is more complex. We are disconnected from our heart and inner light. Now, transition is both a maturation and an awakening process. We need to awaken to our integrity. our authentic self, our inner light. When we are disconnected from who we truly are there is a loss of integrity, peace of mind, and courage. We believe what the media or governments are telling us, even though our heart says something different. There is great peace of mind in feeling the connection to our inner light.

Integrity means not necessarily conforming to societal norms. We listen to others, and we trust our own path. The word courage comes from the French word *coeur*, meaning 'heart.' Heart and soul are terms that often refer to the same essence. To live a soulful life is to live a courageous life. Soul is the essence of who we are. Our inner light creates a body to inhabit to live in and encounter certain experiences and lessons on the earthly plane. Our soul sets up challenges to meet and learn from. Some of these challenges originate in other lifetimes. Everything is meant to be a learning experience.

This is not to say that the earthly plane is part of some cosmic school. Learning is not meant to be serious and hard. Often, we learn the most when we are having fun and taking life lightly. Often, we learn the most when we are curious, engaged, focused, and purposeful. We learn the most when we feel loved and loving. The most powerful force in the universe is love, and when we are connected to our inner light we know this in blood and bone. Our inner light is part of the universal light. Love is a force that transforms everything.

A transition has much to teach us about love. Yet in this timeframe, there is much fear and confusion about love and spirituality. There are so many ideas and belief systems and power games played with the realm of soul. This is because the earthly plane is passing through a time of great ignorance and darkness about spirituality. This is why so many feel confused about spirituality. The net result is that when we feel disconnected from soul we feel contracted, hardened, and afraid. Connection to soul is not a theoretical matter; it must be experienced in the mind and body to be truly known.

A transition helps us break through our fearful, hardened heart so that we can feel and breath the light of spirit once again. Transitions are where life shifts in powerful and unexpected ways. A transition is defined by the dictionary as a 'passage from one form, state, style or place to another.' Implicit in this definition is a process of transformation. Transitions cause us to mature emotionally and mentally so that we can cope with living in a complex world. They involve a whole psychological process.

Transitions help us deconstruct a rigid and self-critical ego. Ego could also be called our personality. Our personality is really a gestalt of subpersonality parts. Problems come when our ego is too small a container for our inner light. Our personality can deny or resist the inner light. This creates certain problems and shuts down experiences and inner abilities that would otherwise be made available.

When most people talk about the ego, they are usually referring to inner aspects that seek to keep us safe, contracted, and shut down. The ego was not designed to be closed and fearful. We are training it to be that way. A connected, happy, aware, and awake ego is not really a problem. We need an ego to contain our inner light. Ego is there for a purpose. The problem with ego is usually that it is just too anxious, closed, defended, armoured, or rigid. The ego is taught to believe in dualistic paradigms of superiority/inferiority and worthiness/unworthiness. The ego is taught to believe that chasing and acquisition is the path to happiness. The ego is taught to believe in looking good. The ego is taught that real genius is cultivated within a Masters or PhD program rather than in the University of Life. The ego is taught to be independent/self-reliant or a whining victim/martyr. The ego is not something we can change through reading a book. The ego has to be transformed, and a radical set of life experiences is one way this can happen.

> *When faced with a radical crisis, when the old way of being in the world, of interacting with each other and with the realm of nature doesn't work anymore, when survival is threatened by seemingly insurmountable problems, an individual life-form — or a species — will either die or become extinct or rise above the limitations of its condition through an evolutionary leap.*
>
> — *ECKHART TOLLE*

There is nothing obvious about transitions. They can sneak up on us without us realizing, and they can begin in strange ways and be accompanied by an odd undercurrent of tension. How we deal with this undercurrent of tension is all-important as it determines the overall experience of the journey. A transition will strip away everything nonessential and help us question everything we know about ourselves and our place in the world; therefore, a transition is often confronting and challenging. It brings us face to face with our deepest dreams and our deepest wounds. Personal transitions help us dig deep within ourselves to find a renewed sense of inner light and purpose.

Transitions are both random and predictable. Once the journey starts, within a certain parameter anything can happen. The journey contains elements of chaos, uncertainty, and surprise. This is how is must be. We cannot control the journey, which means we have to find qualities such as faith and trust to successfully navigate the way ahead.

Transition is a soulful journey; it is also a heroic one (one that is far simpler than the many complex theories derived from Joseph Campbell's original and innovative research and thinking on the mythological hero's journey). The journey is soulful because it returns us to our original essence. The journey is heroic because it will push us into new experiences and it will open our hearts—and in some cases crack them open, revealing inner abilities, gifts, and talents that were previously dormant.

A big transition kicked off for me between the death of my father in January 1991 and the ending of my marriage in October 1993. During that period, I experienced a form of awakening that propelled me into a spiritual path, a new relationship, and a whole new career a few years later. This was my first experience of a spiritual transition in which I felt reconnected to my inner light. Many spiritual teachers entered my life, and many things seemed open to me. This was also my first experience of multi-layered synchronicity. Within the first six months, I had met many of the spiritual teachers who would influence me for the next 15–20 years.

After this transition, I entered into a loving, long-term relationship, found a new career path that I absolutely loved, and was engaged in spiritual practice that felt deep and transformational. So I thought I was just about done with transition. From here on in, life was about gently coasting and enjoying the view. Then, in early 2010, something happened—a trigger was released, someone entered my life, and soon afterwards I had a kundalini awakening experience.

What followed was unexpected, dramatic, and beyond intense. I was thrown into unfamiliar territory, and for the first time in many years I felt anxious, confused, and afraid. This personal transition took me on a roller-coaster ride for three years. I was not sure whether I would survive, and there was one occasion I almost did pass through the veils to the other side. This transition ended when I finished the final draft of this book. Although I stand now on the other side, so to speak, the resonance and impact of my journey will continue, I am sure, for many years to come.

> *Men are not free when they are doing just what they like.*
> *Men are only free when they are doing what the deepest self likes.*
> *And there is getting down to the deepest self! It takes some diving.*
> — *D. H. LAWRENCE*

The Power of Transition

Transitions begin with some form of discomfort. We may realize something important is missing in our lives and start to reflect on what to do about it. A transition may represent an unfulfilled dream that wants to be actualized. A transition may come to remind us of some core values we are not living. The issue here is that we may be so muddled or busy with life that we do not stop to give any of these things a second thought. A transition does not go away because we are too busy for it. A transition begins as tension builds and eventually erupts in our lives, upsetting our plans and routines. Transitions help us release limiting aspects of our past and help us step towards a more positive and life-affirming future. Transitions help us redefine how and where we belong in the world. They push us out of our tight comfort zones and force us into drawing upon inner resources we did not know existed before. A wizard such as Gandalf can come along and knock upon our Hobbit hole door. We might not like the call to adventure, but it has come nevertheless. Our response to the call will influence the kind of journey that follows. It might feel like a walk through a gorgeous place you have never been before, or it might feel like being pushed into deep waters and then told to swim. Whichever way we go, we get to know ourselves as resourceful human beings. The path itself helps to reveal our thus far unknown and untapped potential. Dormant inner potential in human beings is a powerful force. There are gifts within us all that demand life.

When Jesus was on the earthly plane, he spoke of the parable of the sower. In the parable, a farmer went out to sow some seeds. As he was scattering the seed, some fell along the path, and the birds came and ate it. Some fell on rocky places, where the soil was shallow. The seeds sprouted, but when the sun came up, the plants were scorched, and they withered because they had no root. Others fell among thorns, which choked the plants. Some seeds fell on good soil. They came up, grew, and produced a bountiful crop. Similarly, there are seeds within us waiting to burst into life. In our current reality, perhaps the conditions are not right for the seeds to awaken; perhaps our current work or relationship or home is not conducive to the seeds coming to life. A transition takes us away from our current reality and moves us to where the conditions are right for a bountiful crop.

To add to the parable, we do not always know what kind of seeds exist within the soil of the psyche. We are unique beings, and our gifts are unique. Acorns will not grow into violets, nor should they try. There are seeds of many kinds. When these inner seeds break above ground, we start to know whether we are growing an apple tree or violets. This is part of the great mystery of transition. When a seed is activated, its essence can find many outlets. For instance, creativity can manifest in dancing, gardening, painting, poetry, or writing. If we never take the journey, and instead, stay in a narrow bandwidth of existence, then we never discover what we are truly capable of being and becoming in this lifetime.

Dormant Inner Potential

Within each one of us there are seeds of higher potential. Here are some of the most common seeds activating in many people across the planet right now:

ARTIST: The artist is here to awaken to creativity, spontaneity, play, and fun. The artist is at home with writers, poets, singers, dancers, and actors. The artist can be found in the business world and in the home. The artist is not naturally serious but light; he or she knows that joyful flow is the natural order of life. Many people were, and continue to be, discouraged from following a creative path because it does not lead to a proper job. The challenge of this theme is to apply creativity to every area of life.

AWAKENER: Awakeners are the catalysts for radical change. When we awaken and stabilize a high vibration of light in our energy fields, then this stimulates those around us. Awakeners carry catalytic codes of light and stimulate others by their words and presence. Awakeners work in any field of endeavour that needs more light. They work through different means and are drawn to coaching, facilitation, personal development, public speaking, and writing. The awakener is here to learn about the true nature of power.

DREAMER: This life theme is about dreaming new possibilities for your life and the earth. We create reality from the inside out. This awakens the ability to dream new realities for other people. It is said that this ability was very active on the earth in the time of Lemuria. When enough dreamers incarnate on the planet, this is how Heaven on Earth will come into being.

GUARDIAN: A guardian is a life theme that comes to serve in a major way. Many guardians are parents serving the waves of high-vibrational souls being born on this planet at this time. These souls have a strong connection to their inner light, but they often suffer turbulence as they grow up because of the dense vibrations here. Many guardians are here to work with the mineral, plant, and animal kingdoms. They act as advocates for those with no voice.

HEALER: The healer usually works with the old Bible saying "Physician heal thyself." Healers often begin their work because of a healing crisis of some kind. The healer works with people to clear their physical, emotional, mental, and spiritual bodies. The healer can work in many ways. A smile or a hug or a loving thought is healing. Through their radiant presence they know how to uplift and heal others. The healer can also work through the spoken word and energy. The healer also works with the earth, to clear and open energy lines and sacred sites that have been distorted over time.

HERO: The hero is a common theme for many people right now. There are forces in the world that seek to keep us playing small in life. We are here to learn to find courage in following our own path. Fear is the adversary of the hero. They are here to transform weakness into strengths, such as unworthiness into capability and self-deprecation in self-appreciation. This theme helps us learn courage, determination, faith, and perseverance. The hero learns to be resourceful by facing their fear and stepping towards the unknown. The hero is here to learn about facing their fears and finding their heart.

INNOVATOR: The innovator invents and improves. Innovators think outside the box and synergize ideas and information in new ways. They embrace diversity and love people who can challenge their worldview. In this way, they can come up with something new. Innovators are at the cutting edge of the Virtual Information Revolution. The Innovator is here to experiment, network, and follow their unconventional way of thinking and approach to life.

LEADER: The true leader inspires from the front. The true leader has broken through old models of command and control. True leadership is not about telling others what to do; it is about strength, motivation, and power that serve rather than dominate. The challenge of every leader is learning to transform their ego to serve the light. A true leader is a natural communicator who inspires others to find and actualize their inner light.

LOVER: The lover experiences the truth that love heals all. This is a tantric path, where we learn that real vulnerability and gentleness is true power. The lover has to learn to release certain emotions and express others. Certain emotions can be challenging. Growing up in a loveless family is a common challenge for the lover. In life, the lover is often challenged by abandonment, rejection, and loss. The lover is here to learn about love without attachment and with equanimity.

MAGICIAN: The magician works with vision, intention, thought, and feeling. Magicians understand experientially how to attract, shape, influence, and create their experience in this world. The magician works with the mind—primarily belief, imagination, and focus. The magician also works with energy and vibration. The challenge of the magician is to remember to create in the spirit of joy and service. The magician is here to work with power in service to the whole.

SAGE: The sage explores pure light and beingness. The sage sees beyond the duality of good and bad, positive and negative, friends and enemies—they see only unity. The sage may be challenged at various stages by the illusion and pain of ego separation. In this challenge, they learn about the illusions of the world and are reborn. They think, feel, and speak from a place of unity consciousness. The sage is here to reconnect others to the sacred unified field of life.

SYNERGY: Patriarchal systems have suppressed the feminine through war, religion, politics and economics for thousands of years. The divine feminine knows itself through love, holding sacred space, and relating. This theme is allowing women to awaken to their essential core and burst through outmoded ways of expressing feminine sexual and nurturing energy. For men, this quality is about bursting through old stereotypes of masculine energy. This means embracing issues around power and vulnerability in a new way. The divine masculine seeks to know itself through focus, purpose, and action. This is not about being an effeminate New Age man, nor is it about being a Macho Man. There is a middle way, one which many men are finding right now. This seed is about finding inner unity, synergy, and balance.

TEACHER: The teacher is interested in knowledge but is more interested in wisdom. A true teacher helps to wake up the light in others. Teachers learn from their own experience rather than from being told the right way to do things. They teach in a variety of ways, which can include poetry, music, and storytelling. They are skilled in turning complexity into simplicity. A teacher is drawn to sharing ideas that empower others; they do not simply force-feed facts. Teachers are often mavericks, innovators, and synthesizers. The teacher is here to learn about helping others find their own true path in life.

> *The planet does not need more 'successful' people; the planet desperately needs more peacemakers, healers, restorers, storytellers, and lovers of all kinds.*
>
> — *DALAI LAMA*

Transition and the Return of Global Soul

Personal transition is linked to a much larger process, that of global transition. I believe we stand together at a powerful and crucially important crossroads in human history. One way leads to a powerful evolution and flowering of soul and consciousness; the other leads to more ego, control, contraction, and even possibly global tyranny. The planet has been disconnected from the inner light for thousands of years. There are powerful systems and forces in the world that are both intentionally and unintentionally blocking spiritual evolution on this planet. This is all part of the hard game of duality. We grow through opposition to the light.

This is now all changing. Currently, there is much light impacting the planet, and we are being called to awaken to a new resonance of love, cooperation, and sustainable abundance. There are many high-vibrational souls being born on the planet right now. Cosmic forces are aligning to support great movement and change on our planet. Light is hitting old systems that are disconnected from light.

These systems all started off with good intentions and then strayed from that path. This is because any major system within this plane of duality inevitably evolves a prime directive of self-protection. Medical systems will close ranks to protect their own, even at the cost of patients' health and well-being. The Catholic Church closed ranks to protect priests who had abused members of their flock. Pharmaceutical firms demand laws prohibiting complementary health services and products. Politicians close ranks around government spying agencies quoting 'national security.' Wealthy bankers devise new ways to get around laws of the land prohibiting profiteering and excessive bonuses.

Systems that are disconnected from the light create varying degrees of great harm and suffering. These systems encourage disconnection on the planet, and when we feel blocked from knowing the light within, we suffer. Up to a point, suffering is useful if it forces growth. Humanity has now gone way beyond that point, and growth demands our participation. We need to grow up and find a maturity to do things differently on Planet Earth. These old disconnected systems are in dire need of reinvention or renewal.

There are four systems in particular that I want to mention here.

1. DOGMATIC RELIGION

For too long here in the West, we have had to contend with dogmatic and authoritarian Christianity. The original message and mission of Christianity contained much power and light, but this light has faded over time and has now virtually gone out. The original message of Christianity was revolutionary and transformational. The Church (meaning the whole array of traditional churches that teach the message of Jesus the Christ) no longer understands or teaches the essential intended message; rather, it promotes weird and distorted ideas, such as: we were thrown out of the Garden of Paradise; we were born in sin rather than innocence; bad people go to hell; we should fear a judgemental punishing father creator that dwells in some abstract heaven (rather like some absentee landlord). In the absence of a meaningful God, the world becomes the province of the Devil.

None of this ever made much sense to me. Because of its rather warped ideology and message, Christianity has a long history of blocking free thinking, as shown by the cases of Copernicus, Galileo, and Giordano Bruno (the latter burnt alive). Religion has for too long been involved in politics, power games, and wars—the very opposite intention of Jesus' revolutionary message of love. This started under the Roman Emperor Constantine and has been going on ever since. The Church had sidelined women and established a male-dominated priesthood. Women are not allowed to hold high office. The Church is still coming to terms with a past that includes mass murder during the 'burning times' in Europe (mostly of women), when it encouraged a mass hysteria around witchcraft.

The scar of this tragedy, I feel, still haunts Europe today. The Church is struggling to remain relevant in the modern world. The faithful are the unquestioning. The younger generation is not flocking to the Church. Most young people realize that the message of the Church around love, soul, God, and the nature of reality makes little sense in the modern world and does not work in practice.

The Church encourages a denial of the body, which in turn leads to suppression and control of sexual energy. It also has long encouraged the suppression of anger and natural aggression. (I worked within the walls of an urban church for 12 years and so speak from some experience.) The church is out of step with what many people now demand from a modern spiritual path. There are some signs that the Church is in the process of reinvention, but it is still early days. We can but pray that the Church will find its true heart, reinvent itself, and align with the original message of Christ. Only then will it become a trustworthy vehicle once more for radical and revolutionary love.

2. NARROW-MINDED SCIENCE

Science has helped us break away from the worst aspects of dogmatic religion; it has also given us great advancements and technologies. Yet at the same time, science is mostly cold, clinical, unfeeling, anti-heart, and anti-light. Scientists are now the new high priests of the new religion of materialism. This priesthood tells us: there is no reality but material reality; consciousness is a by-product of the brain; nature is fascinating but purposeless; spiritual phenomena can always be explained rationally and when they can't be, they should be ignored.

Science is not interested in things that do not fit its theories, such as when a person has a miracle cure. Science is not interested in our feelings or intuitions or preferences; it is only interested in objective facts. Science does not believe in the human spirit or in a greater universal intelligence, even though it is impossible to disprove either. Science has developed a rigid philosophy that believes in only what it can measure and evaluate. Fundamentalist science is arrogant. How do we know this? Well, we only have to look at the stockpiles of highly destructive weapons around the world to work that one out! Science is the methodology and 'intelligence' behind the pharmaceutical industry that creates more drugs to combat illness and disease, yet we live in a world where we are less healthy than our grandparents.

Pharmaceutical drugs, in many cases, interfere with the energetic workings of the body. There are subtle energy pathways in and beyond the body that science has no knowledge of or interest in. Science tells us that physical matter is all that matters. It has no way of understanding love, except as chemicals swirling around the body. If you want to know more about fundamental science, then you only need read *The Science Delusion* by controversial author and biologist Rupert Sheldrake, who is best known for his work on what he calls 'morphic resonance.' I believe the day will come when science and spirituality will eventually meet and complement each other. That day is perhaps not so far off.

3. BIASED EDUCATION

Education, like science, has brought many benefits, and we mostly agree that education is a good thing. The problem with education is that it is strongly biased in favour of logic, rationality, memory, and left-brain intellect. In so doing, it relegates the heart and right-brain abilities such as intuition, imagination, and vision to the position of poor relatives. Our intellects have been turned into some kind of duelling sword that argues, critiques, debates, and probes for weakness. In the process, so much is thrown out. That includes real emotional intelligence, which allows us to feel a range of responses, such as compassion, and helps us to relate meaningfully with others.

Is it any wonder that so many children find school so unbearable? Research has found high levels of anxiety, depression, and general cynicism among children and adolescents from middle-class and upper-class families, where parents insist on sending children from one learning activity to another. Personally, I believe that when education starts to destroy the curiosity and creativity of children, then it can no longer say it is truly educating. Education is about so much more than making us nice little cogs for work further down the line. It is about developing real thinking, which is not just about a razor-sharp intellect.

Our left-brain faculties seem at war with our right brain. There are those who rebel and embrace right-brain faculties over the left, but this is just the flip side of the coin. Education in the future, I believe, will be about developing both sides of the brain and creating a learning environment that nurtures a synergy of the two. Only then will we generate real genius and wisdom on the planet. The world is full of 'educated' people who have no concept of sustainability or peace. Developing the left brain in favour of the right is a sure formula for developing a strong inner critic. As most people on the spiritual path know, a strong critical ego is a major block in knowing the inner light. Only when education of the many becomes more holistic in its approach will it become a force for real intelligence, wisdom, and empowerment.

4. HEARTLESS CAPITALISM

Last, but certainly not least, is capitalism—the most insidious and most resilient of the lot. Behind all other forces lies the influence of big money. Capitalism is the private ownership of goods and services for profit. There is nothing wrong with this, except that the game rules of private ownership are not fair. Not everyone has equal access to possibility, opportunity, and advancement. There are all kinds of rules and restrictions that favour certain groups over others. The real issue is that capitalism is based on debt and scarcity. Also capitalism never really saw the point in having a heart, unless it could make money out of it!

Heartless capitalism promotes tremendous inequality, since it allows and encourages a very large percentage of assets and money to be in the hands of a small group of people. Heartless capitalism, therefore, promotes self-interest over the collective good. A core belief in capitalism is that everyone is motivated out of self-interest. This ignores the fact that human communities thrive more from a sense of cooperation than competition, which tends to be more destructive than creative in nature,

Capitalism sells us the lie that happiness is just a purchase away; thus, we have a collective madness of chasing and competing for anything of value. We will even destroy the planet to make a quick buck. Heartless capitalism puts a price on everything—joy, sex, children, health, and well-being.

For centuries, we have placed a high value on industrialization and a low value on human communities and nature. This is why we are destroying rainforests and other precious wild habitats. Heartless capitalism is behind those corporations that dominate any profitable industry on the planet, such as pharmaceuticals, energy, or weapons. The system seeks to maintain the privileges of the few over the many. The Occupy Movement created the slogan 'WE ARE THE 99%,' which has made us more aware of the social costs of maintaining our existing economic systems.

Heartless capitalism does not create abundance; rather, it creates poverty and is often a primary cause of war. With a top-heavy population of 7 billion, our planet's increasing demand for goods, services, and resources places us on a dangerous path. Author and scientist Ervin Lazlo suggests our generation is the first in history that can decide whether it is the last in history! What we need are economic systems that serve the whole of humanity, not just a select few. When capitalism shifts, then it is likely that all other systems on the planet will shift. A revised capitalist system needs to serve and connect rather than enslave and disconnect. When this happens, and one day it will, then our planet will wake up from its dark night of ignorance, inequality, scarcity, and greed.

> *On the surface of the world right now there is war and violence and things seem dark. But calmly and quietly, at the same time, something else is happening. Underground, an inner revolution is taking place, and certain individuals are being called to a higher light. It is a silent revolution—from the inside out, from the ground up. This is a Global operation, a Spiritual Conspiracy. There are sleeper cells in every nation on the planet. You won't see us on the TV. You won't read about us in the newspaper. You won't hear about us on the radio. We don't seek any glory. We don't wear any uniform. We come in all shapes and sizes, colours and styles. Most of us work anonymously. We are quietly work-ing behind the scenes in every country and culture of the world—cities big and small, mountains and valleys, in farms and villages, tribes and remote islands. You could pass by one of us on the street and not even notice. We go undercover. We remain behind the scenes. It is of no concern to us who takes the final credit, but simply that the work gets done. Occasionally, we spot each other in the street. We give a quiet nod and continue on our way...*
>
> *— ANONYMOUS BLOGGER*

Light Is Unstoppable

Our planet is in a process of radical transition. This cannot be stopped. All of our old systems are being shaken up right now. Thankfully, in the West, religion no longer has the power to negatively influence us as it once did. There is an emerging interest in the original teachings of Jesus as spoken in the language of the time, Aramaic. This holds the key for Christianity to return to its original sacred roots. Similarly, for decades, science has been influenced by the revolutionary thinking and theories of quantum physics. Films like *What the Bleep Do We Know?* indicate that more high-profile scientists are willing to speak publicly about the synergy of science and mysticism.

Thankfully, education is beginning to embrace teaching methods that show an appreciation for a range of learning styles and intelligences. Alternative education systems such as Waldorf education, developed by anthroposophist Rudolf Steiner, greatly encourage a connection to the inner light. Waldorf education and other alternatives are not available to everyone, and cost can be a prohibiting factor for many families. I also believe that some of the methodologies need updating to make them more relevant for living in the modern world. Capitalism, as it is being practised right now, is like the 'evil' magician Sauron's magical ring, made in the dark to bind and control all the rest. Because of the light impacting the planet, financial systems are wobbling badly.

On a positive note, many heartfelt entrepreneurs are calling for more a conscious, values-led capitalism. In my view, even this does not go far enough, as the very fabric of the debt-based system must change. (For more on this, I recommend reading *Sacred Economics* by Charles Eisenstein.) This complete revision of our debt-based system will open the way for new systems that actively support and promote human communities and the use of sustainable resources.

The good news is that change is already upon us. As we know, many people are saying no to war. Many people are standing up for the rights of the underprivileged. Millions of people right now are exploring alternative lifestyles that take into account the finite resources of our blue-green planet. Millions of people are turning to meditation and alternative healing methods. New solutions and ways of living are emerging daily. These solutions are being spread at rapid speed around the globe by the Internet.

Dr. Clare Graves, the inspiration behind the Spiral Dynamics systemic model, says of this time: 'The present moment finds our society attempting to negotiate the most difficult, but at the same time the most exciting transition the human race has faced to date. It is not merely a transition to a new level of existence, but the start of a new movement in the symphony of human history.'

Now we are almost at the birthing stage. What happens in the next 10–20 years or so will be pivotal to the whole process. The world needs us to change so that the world can change; we are not separate from the world. The only real revolution that can ever work is one that starts from the inside out. If we cannot find peace in ourselves, how can we help promote peace in the world? If we cannot find light in ourselves, how can we offer anything but darkness to the world? Transition is moving us not towards some phoney or contrived New World Order; rather, we are moving into a great shift in consciousness. This is nothing short of a return to Sacred Unity across the planet.

YOUR INNER LIGHT MEDITATION

When you are ready take a moment to stop, relax, and enter into silence. When you feel open and relaxed, begin to focus on your heart and with each in-breath imagine you feel more relaxed.

Feel your connection to the earth. Imagine roots growing out from your feet and down into the core with each cycle of breath. Feel these roots passing through earth, rock, water, and fire to connect with the crystalline core of the earth. Breathe up light from the core of the earth into every cell of your body. In this light, remember you are a child of the earth, you have a right to be here, and this is your home for this lifetime.

Imagine you can breathe the liquid light of the morning sun into a centre of light located in your heart. As you breathe in this light, imagine filling this part of your body with pure liquid light. Allow this light to build and radiate to every cell of your body.

If there is anywhere in your body that feels tense or heavy, imagine you can breathe solar light into it. As you breathe light into this place, notice how the light displaces old energy. Allow any old energy to escape back to the sun to be transformed into pure energy once again.

Keep doing this exercise until you feel lighter and you feel the birth of a mini sun inside you. Notice the radiance of this inner light, and keep building the inner sun until you feel full and overflowing.

With the cycle of your breath begin to focus on this mini sun and feel as though you are moving right into its centre. Imagine that you are this liquid light and that it is expanding to fill every cell of your body. Allow this light to be absorbed by the cells of your bones and blood.

Imagine that this inner liquid light can expand into your heart and emotional field. Allow this light to be absorbed into anywhere you feel anger, fear, shame, or grief. Allow the light to open up and release any stuck or trapped energy.

Imagine this inner light can expand into your mind. Allow this light to be absorbed into your stream of thoughts, as well as your old beliefs and assumptions about life. Allow this light to infuse every thought you have about yourself and your world.

Make friends with this light, and welcome this light as your Higher Self. This light has the power to completely transform you and your life from the inside out. Feel this light overflowing into your aura and out into your reality.

When you are ready, just come back to your cycle of breath. As you come back to this world, keep feeling the light inside you. Allow this liquid light to continue to radiate out into your reality throughout your day.

Throughout your day, take the time to remember and feel the solar light within you. Radiate this light out into the world and allow your reality to shift with love.

2

A Question of Gravity

Many centuries ago, Siam (now modern-day Thailand) was threatened with war. This news reached a monastery in the north of the country that possessed a statue of the Buddha made of solid gold. The statue was quite large, being over 10 feet tall and weighing around 5 tons. The monks could not carry the statue, so they came up with the idea of concealing it with clay before abandoning the monastery. None of the monks returned—perhaps they were all killed—and so the statue stayed hidden for many centuries.

Then, in the mid-1950s, the monastery housing the statue had to be relocated to make room for a new highway. The monks arranged for a crane to come and move the statue to a new location, but it was much heavier than expected and as it was lifted by a crane it began to crack. The statue was lowered back down. Then it began to rain heavily, and so the monks covered the statue.

Later, in the dark of night, the head monk took his flashlight and went out to make sure the Buddha was adequately covered. When the light of the flashlight shone into the crack of the clay, he saw a glimmer, a reflection of something underneath. He found some tools and started to remove shards of clay, only to find that the glimmer grew brighter. Hours later, with all the clay removed, the head monk stood in the presence of a Buddha made of solid gold. This sacred statue stands to this day in Thailand in The Temple of the Golden Buddha.

● ● ●

Soul and consciousness form one side of the transition equation; on the other is our biology. The soul is not separate from the body—the body is the soul in temporary physical form. In the early years, as the body grows and develops, the soul gradually takes more control over the nervous system and brain. At a certain point, we cannot separate body and soul while we are alive. Yes, the soul can leave the body and journey through the various planes of existence in sleep and meditation, but essentially the two coexist to allow us to explore this physical world.

Without consciousness, the body is nothing but an empty shell. People in a coma usually have very little soul light in the body keeping all the vital organs running. They are off elsewhere, having other adventures until it is time to come back or release the body. Consciousness without a physical body cannot experience this world. While in a body, soul is the inner light that animates our outer life. Soul is much greater than one lifetime can handle, since the soul is active on many planes of existence at once. This plane offers many opportunities because of the density here and the timeframe we are in.

Only a few rare individuals have opened up to the whole potential of their soul light in this plane. Such beings we call 'master souls.' On the planet right now, there are but a handful. When you meet such a one, the light coming from them is palpable. These beings do not have to remain in this world; they do so out of love and selfless service for humanity. Many new souls are being born here that can hold a higher frequency of light. These beings are here to help birth a new world. Humanity, for the most part, is unable to hold much light. If the full power of our soul suddenly entered the body, the nervous system would be seriously compromised. This is changing, as more light hits the planet and more people open up to the sacredness of life.

When light enters the body at a rate that is fast yet tolerable, we can call this a spiritual awakening. We open to more soul light in two ways. The first is through continuous spiritual practice. Meditation, visualization, yoga, pranayama, chanting and self-hypnosis techniques, pure living, and visiting sacred power spots on the earth are examples of ways to open and allow more inner light. The second is by passing through a transition process. Staying with the first for a moment: it is unfortunate that religion has long taught that we should idealize the soul and denigrate the body. There is the rather strange, outdated idea that the flesh and sexual energy is sinful. This has got us into all sorts of trouble over the centuries. We cannot really awaken spiritually as long as we trash the body. The body is a home for the soul, and hurting it makes as much sense as trashing our own bricks-and-mortar home.

At the other end of the spectrum, our modern materialistic society teaches us to disbelieve in the soul and all things spiritual. Instead of honouring the light within, we are taught to worship the body. Women are conditioned to believe that there is a certain standard of beauty that they must attain, and that true worth is measured by external appearances. Naturally, women feel good about honouring the body, but the ridiculous degree to which many women go is feeding the ego pure and simple. Men are conditioned to believe that self-worth is measured by earning ability and being a good provider. Men can feel good driving a certain kind of car or dating a certain type of woman because these equate with status and success.

Happiness does not come from a new hairdo or a new sports car. All such ideas, and more like them, lead to a dead end on many levels. Nature grows the body, but we may not fully grow with it. We may become a man or woman and still have the heart and mind of an adolescent. We may grow but stay closed to any spiritual opening or development.

When life becomes closed or stuck, then the soul can encourage, provoke, or support a transition through cosmic time. The intelligence of the body is in tune with all major astrological alignments of the planets in our solar system and stars far beyond. We are not separate from the universe that surrounds us. This is not about fate or destiny, but about a number of forces working deep within us. How we respond to those forces is up to us. We can embrace them or run in the opposite direction. But moved we will be. There are a number of preset astrological transit points we must pass through. Some of these are highly personal and designed to activate our soul potential, while some are more about collective awakening.

A transition can open us on many levels, one of which is to let more soul light into the body. Transitions activated by cosmic or astrological time tend to be more profound psychologically. Deep forces are at work in the psyche, revealing old, blocking energetic patterns and helping us open and move forward in new ways. This is not usually an easy time, but it is a transformative time. Transitions have different degrees of magnitude. When a transition is activated by both cosmic and biological time, then a big transition is initiated. Here, we can expect a radical ride leading to a great opening; after this, nothing in life will ever be the same again.

Conception

Many spiritual teachers say the soul chooses the circumstances of birth, including the time, place, and parents or guardians. This is something that has to be mostly taken on faith, although it makes more sense to me than the idea of birth being a random event like rolling a dice and hoping for the best.

Of course, the idea that there is a soul is also a matter of faith. There are other terms for soul, such as 'pure awareness' or 'higher consciousness.' Soul is not something we possess; rather, it is the truth of our being. We could say that the soul possesses a body, rather than the other way around. There is much that could be said on the subject of conception and consciousness. For now, I will simply say that the state and level of consciousness of the parents making love to conceive a child is important. As a rule of thumb, the more love and consciousness involved in the sexual union, the higher the vibration of the incoming soul.

Birth to Adolescence

Birth is our first transition. Some psychologists even compare it to a form of heroic journey. Even though the passage from womb to this world is unconscious (we do not yet possess conscious faculties to remember this journey), nevertheless, I agree with those who say that our time in the womb and the manner of our birth sets the context for our lives—not only the experience of birth itself but the circumstances of birth: the time, the place, the family, the culture, and the astrological configurations.

Into this mix is (hopefully) added the extra ingredients of the parents' love and care, which in the first developmental stage is vitally important, especially the mother's positive and ongoing loving caring for the child. This care is greatly influenced by how loved and cared for the mother feels in her family and community. Here, constant touch and visual contact are crucially important. If this happens, then we safely grow in the confidence that we are loved and cared for and we trust that life is basically okay. If we fail to experience love, and our needs are not really met, we tend to feel unsafe and unworthy until shaken loose by a transition process, or by some other means.

In this early stage of life, we are not only learning to manage our physical body—walking, talking, feeding, and toilet training—but also adopting unconsciously many patterns from our family. These patterns do not just relate to our parents but also to grandparents and great grandparents, and beyond. During this time, we can take on any number of limiting programs, such as anxiety, shame, guilt, and self-criticism. German psychotherapist Bert Hellinger, the father of Family Constellations therapy, once said, "Children unconsciously aspire to equal their parents in suffering."

Of course, this is only part of the picture, for as we get older (3–5 years of age), we are also learning about life through play and by constructing different scenarios in our internal make-believe worlds. Later (6–11 years of age), we learn about interacting with other children and then we are exposed slowly but surely to learning about academic demands, competence, and success. The psychologist Erik Erikson said that this is when we step on a path of industry or inferiority. Here, we are learning to perform more complex tasks and skills. This is where we learn confidence and capability or learn to doubt ourselves. This time prepares us for the inevitable rush of puberty (12–18 years of age), where we seek to separate from our parents and develop a unique sense of self and identity. Erik Erikson believed this period marked the all-important difference between identity and confusion.

From an astrological perspective, a major transit happens around the age of 15. Here, we experience our first Saturn Opposition, which is where we start making important decisions around study and possibly even career. This time involves a growing crisis of identity, which is never easy but necessary in order to help us gain more space, and ultimately greater independence. This transit moves us to start looking at the big wide world out there. From a spiritual perspective, this time potentially heralds a powerful connection to the inner light. But because our society has forgotten the importance of soul, and no longer has the wisdom to initiate us into adulthood, this important transit is often volatile and unpredictable.

THE ADOLESCENT TRANSIT

Although the adolescent transit offers the possibility of major awakening, what tends to happen nowadays is a great contraction or closing, which makes it is a confusing time of emotional highs and lows for young people. Here, it soon becomes apparent that lots of hormones in the body, plus a lack of real worldly wisdom, do not usually go well together—all made doubly difficult because the teenage brain and nervous system are not yet properly developed. Teenage years are often a time of disconnection from the inner light of soul, rather than a strengthening of the connection. When this happens, we might then vainly seek that connection through addictive behaviour or celebrity culture.

For girls, changes in body shape and menstruation begin around 12 years of age. For boys, the voice deepens, muscles develop, and facial hair starts growing. Mood swings happen, and romantic/sexual feelings start to develop for the opposite sex. There is anxiety or excitement about the prospect of adulthood and concerns about being socially accepted. There are pressures around making choices to do with study or work. There are also the added ingredients of peer pressure and social expectations. Choices made at this time can run for an entire lifetime. Here, we also start to feel the pressure of unhealed family patterns rising to the surface and seeking acknowledgement and resolution. This can be a time of unconsciously rejecting or taking on the values of the parents. Either path can create confusion and internal conflict with their own, as yet unknown, values.

Early Adulthood

Once we pass adolescence we are steadily, or suddenly, thrust into the world of work, money, and relationships. Erik Erikson said that this is where we learn to differentiate between intimacy and isolation. We learn to relate or withdraw, depending on what has happened previously and the manner in which we enter this period. Erikson believed that a rounded sense of self (established during the previous stage) was essential to help us build intimate relationships. If this is not achieved, then we are more likely to suffer from 'isolation, loneliness, and depression.'

For some, there can be a desire to jump into relationships to escape isolation. This does not bode well for the durability or happiness factors in such relationships. Deeper layers of previously hidden family patterns can become activated in this period. Here, we begin to feel the pressure of systemic family patterns. We may have no idea of our family history past our parents, but this does not prevent the soul of the family from exerting its pressure on us. We may find ourselves living out patterns that are not of our making.

In the West, we have many therapeutic methodologies, but most of them focus entirely on the individual and forget the family system they are embedded into. Traumatic events, such as the premature death of a parent, sibling, or child, an abandonment, or loss of a family member through tragic circumstances, can exert a powerful force down through the bloodline.

Family Constellations founder Bert Hellinger spoke about many extraordinary cases that highlight the power of loyalty and systemic guilt that pass down the generations. One such case involved a lawyer who came to see him after researching his family history. The lawyer had discovered that his great-grandmother was married but got pregnant by another man. Her husband died at the age of 27, on December 31, amidst suspicion that he had been murdered. The woman then married the lover. Since that time, three men in the family had committed suicide—all at the age of 27. New Year's Eve was approaching, so the lawyer had gone to his cousin to warn him of the family history. He found that his cousin had already bought a gun intending to shoot himself!

During early adulthood we encounter a very important transition point, which arrives somewhere between the ages of 28 and 30. This transit is where we start to feel an increasing pressure from the soul to align with our values, and as a result make some new decisions in the world. At the very least, this transit comes to shake us up in some way. In psychological speak, this time has been labelled the Quarter Life Crisis. 'Quarter life crises don't happen literally a quarter of the way through your life,' says Dr. Oliver Robinson, a researcher with the University of Greenwich in London. 'They occur a quarter of your way through adulthood, in the period between 25 and 35, although they cluster around 30.'

The research found that the Quarter Life Crisis—which lasts on average for two years—can generally be a positive experience. Dr. Robinson says that such early-life crises can help move a person from feelings of being trapped and be a catalyst for changes that will eventually lead to the building and cementing of a new life.

From an astrological point of view, this transition is known as the Saturn Return, and it is for many a big wakeup call. In my own experience, this was the first time that I felt the pressure of soul and astrological time calling me to a new path. At the time, I had no idea what a Saturn Return was all about. This transit shook up everything in the few years that followed, from my long-term relationship to my career, and it also strongly impacted and opened up my spiritual path.

It takes about 29.5 years for slow-moving Saturn to return to its original position in the sky when you were born. When it comes around and hits you, then you can be sure that the reverberations can be felt well into your early thirties. A Saturn Return brings with it a certain pressure of time; it can bring to awareness, perhaps for the first time, a sense of our mortality.

Saturn is a planet associated with the qualities of inner discipline, focus, and clear-sightedness. Saturn is sometimes called 'the rough teacher' or 'the disciplinarian.' This transit is often experienced as a kind of crisis, during which we have to face up to our fears. It can cause a shaking of our foundations, which is good in that it enables us to shake off what's not real. Where a committed relationship has been formed before a Saturn Return, then this transit will shake that relationship and test its durability or happiness. Where a relationship is found wanting, then it will often dissolve at this point. A Saturn Return is a time to take stock of our dreams and consider what it would really take to achieve them. Now is the time to sort out fantasy from reality and figure out what's still possible and then make the necessary changes or adjustments.

This can be a crossroads period, when life-altering decisions can be made. Vincent Van Gogh became a painter instead of a minister at the age of 30. Of course, you do not have to be a celebrity to be touched by a Saturn Return.

I met Dawn at a friend's dinner party on Christmas Eve 2012, and she told me her story. A few years prior, she had felt she was, as she said, the 'centre of the universe … with no real consideration for other people.' At this time, she had an eating disorder, and was heavily into drugs and alcohol.

She was also, she continued, 'career driven and hedonistic and doing lots of partying. I wanted to be wild. Then, just before my 29th birthday, I lost my job, which in hindsight was the best thing that happened to me since it forced me to look at what I was doing. I went into a 12-Step Program, and I met a sponsor and instantly I became abstinent from drink and drugs. It also helped to clear up my bulimia and anorexia problem. My sponsor was very spiritual, and he recommended some spiritual books. I started to meditate, and I felt/saw blue and green light pulsing up and down my spine. That was when I knew there was something very real to everything I was reading in the spiritual books. These experiences led me to completely change my views and my life.'

Middle Adulthood

The next stage happens somewhere between the ages of 35 and 55. This is when we become increasingly occupied with issues of meaning, direction, purpose, and family. This period can be a fruitful time, both materially and spiritually. Erik Erikson said this period was about generativity or stagnation (although he believed this period extended between 40 and 65 years of age).

In this timeframe, there are two important astrological transits that affect everyone. The first is the Uranus Opposition, which comes around 40–42 years of age. The Uranus Opposition lasts a little over a year, and in some cases up to two, but the effects can be felt even longer. This is an awkward time—we aren't old, but we aren't getting any younger, either. This is a time when people assess where they've been and where they're going with an intensity like never before. Some feel that they haven't lived up to their potential. Others think about their future. Should I plan for old age? Should I get married? Am I happy in my marriage? It is a time for reassessment and a time for some home truths that are not always pleasant. The Uranus Opposition can feel like time is running out. It can also herald a new period, when life becomes more open, fluid, and enjoyable.

James described his Uranus Opposition: 'After my 40th birthday, I felt something open inside of me. I cannot really describe the feeling, other than I felt a greater sense of ease. After my 40th birthday, I had the year of my life. I met the partner of my dreams. I also began a new phase in my working life that was to lead to a new level of fulfilment and success.'

The next astrological transition point is around the age of 50. This is what astrologers call the Chiron Return. This is the beginning of the classic midlife crisis. When this occurs, we come face to face with the real reason we are here on this beautiful and challenging planet. My own recent big transition was probably triggered by my Chiron Return. This was the biggest astrological transit to date, much more powerful in many ways than either my Saturn Return or Uranus Opposition.

Davide, a good friend, said that whilst going through his Chiron Return, 'I felt I was losing the plot. It felt like a descent into a very dark hole. I am still waiting to come out the other side.'

THE MIDLIFE TRANSIT

Midlife is a powerful transition time. It can herald a phase of struggle that itself can lead to a renewed sense of meaning and purpose in life. When this phase is successfully navigated, many people find it leads to a new level of creativity, wisdom, and eldership. There is a new level of connection to soul. Life deepens, and there is a strong, durable feeling of authenticity. Where it is not navigated successfully, then there can come the terrible feeling that the journey was not fruitful or beneficial in any way. Signs of passing through a midlife crisis can include:

- Starting to worry about getting old, which can be accompanied by a desire to hang around younger people;
- A desire to get back into good physical shape;
- Needing less sleep;
- A desire to follow old dreams that were ignored or put to one side;
- The feeling of wanting to run away from everything, unexplainable bouts of depression or sadness, irritability or unexpected angry outbursts, and perhaps even the feeling of being trapped;
- The desire to change routines. What seemed interesting before may now seem boring. There may be a re-emerging interest in creativity, perhaps a desire to dance, paint, or write;
- A desire to change one's life completely and an urge to change jobs or partners during this time is common;
- Depending on how we handle things, this time determines whether we turn up the volume on our inner radiance or turn the volume down and stagnate into bitterness, shallowness, and regret.

Late Adulthood

This last stage happens around the age of 55 and onwards, through to retirement and, finally, the last great transition of death. Late adulthood can be a time of tremendous insight and joy, when we look back on our lives with a sense of fulfilment. If we believe we have made a meaningful contribution to life, we reach the stage that Erik Erikson calls Integrity. If we believe we have not achieved this, there are feelings of bitterness, regret, and even despair, instead. The Danish philosopher Kierkegaard observed that the most common kind of despair comes from not being who we truly are and a more powerful form of despair comes from choosing to be something other than our true self.

Late adulthood is a powerful time, when we shift away from a working life towards retirement. This is where we no longer find meaning in work but in other activities. Family can become even more important. For those with children, this was traditionally a time of being a grandparent, but in this time of people having children later in life this is not always the case. In my own case, I have found being a grandparent in my mid-fifties extremely rewarding. I love them dearly and find them so much fun.

Just to give you an idea of what it feels like, in the summer of 2012, I wrote the following poem to my two grandchildren. I had it printed by a designer in white text on a chocolate-brown background. It is now framed and owned by my daughter.

EVA AND BELLA

They love dolls and dresses, DVD's and iPad's,
Face painting and parties, lipstick and shoes.
They love stories and talking, dancing and drawing, singing
And of course they love eating lots of chocolate.

Films keep them quiet, but only for a while –
They love people dancing and singing and doing crazy things.
They drop crumbs on the floor, leave toys in the kitchen, invade Grandma's bedroom, and (everyone agrees) they make a general mess.

They are a flower in the hand, a ball in the sand,
An ache in the back, a squirm in the lap, a lovely afternoon nap.
Every week they go to the park,
Have a go on the jumpy-jumpy,
Where they have a slide and a swing.

They are a quivering lip, a slobbering kiss,
A hot clutching hand and a warm hug.
At the end of the day there is always the evening bath.
What more can I say, except they are both sweet beyond belief.

—LOVE GRANDDAD STEVE

Late adulthood is either a rich and creative time or one of dwindling of meaning, purpose, and usefulness. From an astrological point of view, there is one more major transition spot that comes around between the ages of 58 and 60. This is our second Saturn Return, and it offers a window of deep change and life-changing rewards. This transit offers us the potential to move into wise eldership.

Some years ago, I had the privilege of hearing author and poet John O'Donohue at a talk he gave in London a few years before his death. He spoke of a woman at an Irish wedding, and although John did not mention her age it sounded fairly typical of a second Saturn Return. This was a quiet person, who kept herself to herself. She was married to a wealthy 'upright' person, who everyone around her knew was quite mean and controlling. People who knew the woman would say she always seemed sad.

At the wedding, she had a few drinks and being not so used to alcohol, her normal reserved manner began to slip. The music was playing, and no-one was dancing. Suddenly, she got up on her own and began dancing. It was a wild dance, a mixture of ballet and rock. Everyone watched in silence. She seemed that day to dance out 30 years of captive longing, and the things she could never say or do came flooding out on the dance floor. The onlookers began to shout and clap their encouragement, and she continued on until the music stopped and then she returned to her table. Although blushing, she held her head high, and those around her could see that 'her eyes were glad, and there was a smile beginning around the corners of her mouth.'

Death

The ultimate transition is the fading and demise of the physical body and the release of our light back to the soul planes. Through the gateway of death, we find release, rest, reflection, and the integration of all our earthly life experiences; yet, because the world is spiritually asleep, we are taught to fear death as a terrible enemy. As we approach this transition, we do so either in complete acceptance or regret and fear. Death is the completion of life, and if we have lived fully and true to our mission, then we will pass smoothly through this radical transition. If not, then we will reach this stage and probably look back with disappointment, regret, and despair at all our mistakes and failures.

The Buddha said often that death was his greatest teacher, and he taught his followers to contemplate death as a way of living with more presence in the moment.

One of my favourite spiritual teachers, Seth, spoke on death: 'People die when they are ready to die, for reasons that are their own. No person dies without a reason. You are not taught that, however, so people do not recognize their own reasons for dying, and they are not taught to recognize their own reasons for living…'

We are not taught to view death as an essential part of living; rather, we shun death and the dying in order to maintain the myth that the light bright and beautiful is always best.

In the autumn of 2012, I heard an author called Bronnie Ware speak on the subject of death and the dying. She had spent several years working in palliative care, caring for patients in the last few months of their lives, and recorded their dying epiphanies in a blog called *Inspiration and Chai*. She later published her observations as a best-selling book called *The Top Five Regrets of the Dying*.

The Top Five Regrets of Dying

1. **THE FIRST REGRET**
    I wish I'd had the courage to live a life true to myself, not the life others expected of me.

2. **THE SECOND REGRET**
    I wish I hadn't worked so hard.

3. **THE THIRD REGRET**
    I wish I'd had the courage to express my feelings.

4. **THE FOURTH REGRET**
    I wish I had stayed in touch with my friends.

5. **THE FIFTH REGRET**
    I wish that I had let myself be happier!

In your life—the center of it, not the part for earning a living or the part that gains you notice and credit, or even the part that leads others to like you but in the central self—are feelings so important and personal that the rest of the world cannot glimpse who you are and what is happening, deep in there.

— *WILLIAM STAFFORD*

Transitions and Radical Self-Care

In James Joyce's classic *Dubliners*, there is that wonderful line, 'Mr. Duffy lived a short distance from his body.' In the story, Mr. Duffy is a one-dimensional bureaucrat who lives a boring, plain, and colourless life. He is the stereotypical postmodern man—cut off from his heart, his inner light, and from meaningful relationships, and instead defined by rules and protocols.

If we look hard enough, we can find Mr. Duffy in the world and also lurking in ourselves. For centuries, we have been conditioned to distance ourselves from our bodies and centre ourselves firmly in the head. We have already seen the impact this has on hardening the heart and inhibiting our ability to live whole-heartedly.

When Descartes made his famous statement, '*Cogito, ergo sum,*' meaning 'I think, therefore I am,' there was a gradual movement away from the body and from nature into the mind. But there is no separation between body, mind, and spirit, although we have been taught this way for some centuries now. When we reject the flesh, we also reject our ability to feel deeply.

Feelings are an important way we make sense of the world. Men are usually discouraged from feeling, and women are classed as neurotic or oversensitive for feeling. In Britain, we have a reputation for not expressing our feelings very much. Some years ago, I went to a talk in London by an American energy healer, physicist, and author called Barbara Brennan, founder of the Brennan School of Healing, who was speaking on the subject of healing. She began the talk strangely by asking the question, 'So, how are you feeling today?' The audience sat in silent response, and after a pause, she made the point that in Britain we are more used to thinking about feelings than actually feeling them.

A transition comes to wake us up, and this includes our connection to our physical form and to our feeling self. The radical journey of transition can wake up a whole spectrum of feelings. The journey can also help us extend our ability to feel and also to respond to life in new ways.

The story of the Statue of the Golden Buddha, which I told at the beginning of this chapter, is a great metaphor for the hidden light of the soul in physical form. This authentic self has been called many names. In Buddhism, it has been called 'our original face'; in Christianity, it has been called 'soul' or 'original blessing'; in the New Age, it is called 'higher self' or 'universal mind'; I call it 'the inner light.'

Kabir, a Sufi poet, wrote that, inside this body, 'there are canyons and Pine Mountains, and the maker of canyons and Pine Mountains. All seven oceans are inside, and hundreds of millions of stars.' Beyond the clay of matter, we are one with the same power that sustains the sun, stars, and the complexity of the entire universe. We are just a tiny spark of that all-encompassing power exploring a grand adventure in this moment in time and space.

The great paradox of being spirit in a body is not to deny the body nor mistake it for our authentic eternal self. The self is our conscious awareness, and it is housed within a body that grows. Our body has its own intelligence, which could be thought of as an intelligent servant to our soul or inner light. This servant is aware of cosmic and biological time, but it does not always understand what the soul is trying to achieve. Sometimes, this translates in the body consciousness as both initiating and resisting a transition. We will explore more about this in later chapters.

Suffice it to say for now that if we have experienced difficult transitions in the past, especially in the womb and during birth, then our developing ego-body consciousness will have good reason to resist transition. This is the real paradox of the journey. We will feel a desire to move towards transition and also resist it. The resistance comes from the fact that our developing ego-body consciousness is a survival mechanism that will always seek to get us out of the way when a car is hurtling towards us. The ego-body consciousness deals with fight, flight, or freeze, and is afraid of discomfort, pain, and annihilation.

When a transition hits, and we are taken on a journey into the unknown, it is important to remember that the body is an electromagnetic entity, and much like any electrical appliance it needs to be cared for and grounded properly. Some transitions are particularly rough and then it is common to feel disconnected from our body and be more in the head. In a super-rough transition, caring for the body is particularly important, because the spiritual awakening process can put a considerable strain on the nervous system and the body, in general.

It takes discipline to stay connected to the body before it becomes pleasurable. For instance, walking on wet grass with bare feet is very helpful to stay connected to the grounding forces of nature. Animals also have the ability to help us stay grounded. I have a preference for playing with cats, since they seem to have a natural ability to help us humans stay sensually connected to the earth. Taking time to appreciate colour, sound, and beauty in the world is another way, as is taking the time to enjoy a tasty meal. One gorgeous way to stay grounded and also feel our inner light is to make love slowly with a committed partner with whom we feel genuine connection and love.

When we feel that we live in our own bodies, we feel more present to what is going on around us. Being present means we can handle dramatic change more easily and effectively, and we feel more capable of tolerating risk and uncertainty. When we are in our body and out of our mind, we are not thinking about what should be happening, or worrying about what other people think or what is the right thing to do. Being in the body makes it easier to move slowly without undue haste, even when things get exciting or challenging.

Another reason why it is important to stay connected to the body is that it helps us stay in touch with our intuition. Intuition starts with a good connection with the body, which often comes as subtle physical sensations, such as a feeling in the chest or gut before it becomes a direct message to the mind. For someone locked in the head, warning signals from the body go unnoticed or ignored, until they build up to dangerous levels. I believe sickness and accidents in times of transition can often be avoided by just having a practice of staying connected to the intelligence-wisdom of the body.

RADICAL SELF-CARE

- It is important to generally cut down on all the different types of garbage currently entering your body-mind system.
- Reduce the intake of news and information that just rev up your mind and your fight-or-flight response for no useful purpose. Cut down on the amount of time you watch TV or read newspapers. Only take in essential information.
- Drink plenty of clean pure water. Eat an alkaline diet. Take appropriate minerals, oils, and supplements to maintain a healthy system.
- Wear clothes made from natural materials, such as cotton and wool, since these allow a free flow of energy around the body.
- Slow down and be conscious of what you are doing rather than running on automatic. Take time to stop and smell the roses. Notice each sip of tea, each mouthful of food, each footstep, each subtle movement in washing the dishes.
- Avoid spiritual abstractions and practices that take you out of the body and into the head. Find short periods of time for stillness and silence throughout the day. Practise being mindful. Notice how you feel throughout the day, and when your energy dips or you feel tense, scattered, or

distracted. Meditate on the natural flow of the breath, and use this to stay in the moment. Whenever your mind runs to the past or future or some fantasy, then just bring your awareness back to the breath and the present moment.

- Whenever possible, visit wild places in nature, and walk on the earth barefoot as often as you can. Open your senses, smell the trees, feel the wind or sunshine on your skin, touch the grass and leaves, and listen to the birds and noises of nature.
- Practise meditating at sunrise and sunset. At sunrise, imagine you can breathe the invigorating rays of sunshine into your body and fill yourself with light and energy for the day. At sunset, imagine that you can breathe out and release any energy locked in your body that does not belong to you or needs releasing.
- Practise energy movement therapies such as yoga, tai chi, or aikido. Go for a walk or a swim as often as possible. Dance and sing. Treat yourself to regular steam baths and massage. Some bodywork, such as shiatsu and deep tissue massage, can be very nourishing and healing.
- Practise standing naked in front of a mirror and really look at your body. Witness, touch, and really appreciate your body. Practise sending love and appreciation to those parts of your body that you do not find lovable.
- Learn to appreciate the power of touch. Practise being tactile with others and enjoying appropriate physical connection. Feel the importance of touch, and open to giving and receiving touch and hugs throughout your day.

3

Smooth Transitions

*Alice was getting tired of sitting on the riverbank when suddenly
a White Rabbit with pink eyes suddenly ran past her, the rabbit
muttering to himself, about 'being late!' When the rabbit took out
a pocket watch to check the time, Alice jumped to her feet.
She suddenly realized that she had never seen a rabbit wearing a
waistcoat or one owning a watch before. Burning with curiosity,
she ran after the rabbit just in time to see the rabbit pop down
a large hole under a hedge.
Without thinking she followed, and before she could stop herself
she found that she was suddenly tumbling down a deep well.
Finally, she landed in a long, narrow hallway with many doors
of different sizes. As she explored the hallway, she came across
a three-legged table upon which Alice found a tiny gold key and
a green bottle that said 'Drink me'...*

— *LEWIS CARROLL, ALICE IN WONDERLAND*

The difference between soul and spirit, wrote pioneer therapist Carl Jung, is that spirit is light, joyful, and upward-moving, seeking the light of consciousness, whereas soul is deep dark, downward-moving, seeking wholeness and integration. Transitions can follow quite similar routes: some transitions thrust us downwards, through chaos and crisis, while others sweep us more lightly upwards into adventure. Both have their challenges and gifts, and both are valid and powerful paths of transformation.

This chapter explores the upward sweeping path of smooth transitions. (Please note: if you are going through a challenging transition right now, this chapter does not apply to you.) This emerging path is like Alice, burning with curiosity, chasing the white rabbit across fields, and into a hole and then somehow ending up in Wonderland. We chase a dream and we do not know where it will take us. Then again, sometimes we just stumble into a smooth transition, like Alice, without really thinking too much about it. Yet more often than not there is some degree of volition and conscious choice.

We choose the journey because our current reality does not reflect a desired reality. That desired reality exists in our heart somewhere. Perhaps it's not fully conscious, merely a seed waiting to germinate. But every seed waits to activate and take us on the heroic path of desires, goals, dreams, and visions. Every journey needs a push to get it going. Perhaps the push comes from a desire to leave a confining reality; perhaps the push comes from something more enticing that we want to experience. Fantasies on the other hand do not lead to anything very much. Fantasies are a running away from reality, not a radical engagement with life.

Then again, there are shallow dreams that we want to experience, yet they lead nowhere. We may buy a bigger house, start a new business, or marry a classier or more beautiful person, but life carries on and nothing much changes. There can be moments of pleasure, but these are not long-lived. When the buzz runs off, we are looking for the next fix. This is a form of retail therapy that we may also apply to our friendships, relationships, and other areas of our lives. If we follow shallow dreams, then we close ourselves down at a number of psychological, emotional, and spiritual levels. Such dreams are dangerous because they come from the ego, not the soul. If we continue, it will feel like putting locks on the door and blocking access to our authentic self. This is not a good idea, because then life becomes rather two-dimensional.

Following the dictates of the ego is a sure path to a rough transition, but more about that in the next chapter. For now, all I need say is that a rough transition is like putting a stick of dynamite into our reality to blast away shallow dreams and the ego armour covering our authentic self. A smooth transition does not do this; it is a gentler path of reconnection to our essential nature and core values.

As mentioned before, a smooth transition can emerge from a time of aimlessness, frustration, unhappiness, or disconnection. We recognize that something is amiss and start to explore different ways to do something about it. Thus aimlessness, boredom, frustration, and unhappiness can push us to do something different and change course. Perhaps we take time out to reflect on what is truly important. Perhaps we take time to examine our beliefs and values and clarify what we want to do with our lives.

A smooth transition is also initiated by nurturing and following an important dream. Following a dream is a 180-degree journey in the opposite direction from critiquing, complaining, nitpicking, or even problem-solving at its worst. Rather than focusing on problems, we start to consider goals and possibilities. A goal is fixed; a dream is not. We dream of things that could be. We may plan the journey, but we cannot control the journey. If we could, it would no longer be a transition. In a transition, we get to directly experience the great mystery of a higher force guiding the thrust and direction of our lives. The way of achieving a dream may itself be more incredible than the end result.

Sometimes in life, a first step in faith is required before the next step presents itself. Alice chased the white rabbit across a field and without thinking followed him into a hole, and then the way into Wonderland presented itself. Sometimes, not knowing what is ahead is a good thing. Perhaps Alice would have baulked at the chase if she had consciously known she would fall into something very alien from her current reality.

A dream is focusing on the end result and not worrying at all about how we will get there. Perhaps we want to earn money in a more joyful way, or we want to explore our spirituality in a specific way, or we want to travel around a certain continent. When we focus on the end result, we do not need to know how it will all work out. If the intention and desire are strong we will find a way. The way to every dream is strewn with challenges, because this is the tried-and-tested way we grow. When edging out of our familiarity zone, all challenges we meet make complete sense in light of the adventure being undertaken.

I am free, no matter what rules surround me. If I find them tolerable, I tolerate them; if I find them too obnoxious, I break them. I am free because I know that I alone am morally responsible for everything I do.
— *ROBERT HEINLEIN*

Transition Takes Us Into the Unknown

Every transition moves us beyond the familiar into the scary unknown. This is one of the real differences between transition and change. Change is a rearranging of the furniture of our life, whereas a transition is a move into a new home and different location. Every transition involves a movement out of familiarity. This zone is all we know—what has become familiar, comfortable, and habitual.

The whole notion of comfort zones was popularized by Susan Jeffers in her brilliant book, *Feel the Fear and Do It Anyway*—although, perhaps a better term for this is 'familiarity zone,' because many comfort zones are not that comfortable. We can be familiar with addiction, failure, loss, betrayal, violence, and so on. These are not comfortable, but they are familiar, and we tend to stay with the devils we know rather than go beyond them, out of the fear that even worse scenarios await us.

Some people are very familiar with risk taking, and often real intimacy lies outside the zone. For example, a friend of mine who worked as a corporate coach told me about a client who had climbed several mountains but lacked the courage to ask a woman out on a date. Here, the risk of rejection felt greater than the danger of climbing a mountain. Whatever our familiarity zone, there is always a sense of risk and fear at the edge of our zones.

We all have invisible limits on every quality and experience available on the earthly plane. We place limits on how much joy, love, grace, beauty, or power we allow ourselves to experience. One woman I know has a very loving and generous nature but places a strong limit on the amount of joy she allows herself to feel. Whenever she is in a situation where there is a certain level of laughter, friendship, or happiness, I have witness her sabotage it over and over again, so that the joy recedes and she can feel comfortable again in some pointless drama. I did try to point this out as compassionately as I could, but the feedback was not accepted, and so the limiting cycle continued.

There are many invisible limits we can place, or allow to be placed, on ourselves. Many of these are picked up unconsciously as we are growing up. We can place invisible limits on how much success we will allow ourselves in our career, and how much abundance in the form of money and other good things we will let into our lives. It is not uncommon to believe that love is a finite resource, because love was often experienced in this way in our family. Perhaps, we set limits on play or creativity or adventure. These limits are strong because they are hidden and invisible. We cannot separate reality from our ideas of reality. We believe this is just the way life is and never think to question our invisible beliefs and conditioning.

One of the purposes of a transition is to make the invisible visible. Once we can see that our beliefs about reality are self-fulfilling prophecies, rather than fixed rules about how all life operates, then we can do something about it. Transition is a transformative journey, because it helps us shake off the comfortable unreal and step into the uncomfortable real. When we go beyond our limits of joy, love, intimacy, or play, it can feel scary and exhilarating at the same time.

Even the most timid amongst us can turn into a roaring lion when we follow a path that has heart and power. When we step outside our familiarity zone, the whole thing shifts. No longer is the unknown completely alien. We are now exploring beyond its edges and mapping out the terrain. Outside the familiarity zone, life is no longer mundane and routine. It becomes utterly itself, amazing, challenging, intriguing, inspiring, revealing, and uncontrollably divine.

You must learn one thing,
The world was made to be free in.
Give up all the other worlds...
— DAVID WHYTE

Transition, Motivation, and Freedom

Transition is primarily about freedom, expansion, and a lightening of the ego load. The experience of freedom, or lack of it, comes at many levels. There can be freedom of material resources, such as money, networks, information, and other useful assets. There can be freedom from emotions cycling around, such as anger, fear, guilt, or grief. And there can be mental freedom from restrictors, such as anxiety, doubt, conformity, confusion, duty, or helplessness.

With freedom comes greater choice and flexibility on many levels. Freedom is our birthright, but the conventional world does not always see it that way. There are certain restrictive forces in the world, so to gain our freedom we need a strong motivating and liberating force to break free from the holding gravity of our familiarity zone.

There are two motivating and liberating forces available to us. They are quite obvious and grounded in our everyday experience. The first is pain, and the second is desire. Both create a kind of deep tension that can lead to a smooth transition.

For a moment, let us explore pain. We feel pain in many ways. We feel angry, bored, let down, unfulfilled, or unhappy. Perhaps the pain feels quite intense. This means that the potential for liberation is strong. We may really hate our job, where we are living, or just intensely dislike our rather dull and uneventful life. Pain can lead us to a choice point. If we make a meaningful choice, then we move in time to something more interesting, stimulating, joyful, or graceful. When pain leads to a running away from reality or worse an out-of-the-frying-pan-into-the-fire type of scenario, then we could be heading for a rough transition. When we follow a dream and step into the unknown, anything can happen, and it is usually something magical.

Chrissy was living her dream life, or so she thought. She had a very creative and desirable job working for a record label and TV marketing company, working with high-profile singers and bands. It was a job she had desired for some time, and the opportunity arose and she grabbed it with both hands. She was living with her boyfriend in a beautiful flat in Covent Garden, and although she thought she was happy, deep down something was missing.

She said: 'I convinced myself that my job was more amazing than it really was. I was really just comfortable on the surface. Then I found a spiritual book on channelling and was introduced to other similar books. The more I read, the more it seemed I was removing my blinkers and seeing my life more clearly. I was getting up in the morning, meditating and doing yoga, setting the vibration for the day and then my whole vibe would drop at work. I was coming home with a sore back and sore eyes.

'I prayed for three months for something to happen. At a certain point there was no going back. I knew the job was not right for me. I started applying for contract work. Then, suddenly, I was offered redundancy. Not long after, some contract work came through. Around the same time, I knew it was time to end my relationship. This was a time of big change. I felt this strong purpose, a strong, powerful vibration of where I wanted to be. I started doing some work promoting a spiritual channel I liked and respected.

'I was learning so much, working with people I respected and loved. I was planning and coordinating spiritual events and also speaking with this spiritual channel three times a week. I started some small circles for people interested in this work that would meet in my flat. I also joined another community of really lovely spiritual people that have been so supportive of my journey so far.'

If you let fear of consequence prevent you from following your deepest instinct, then your life will be safe, expedient, and thin.
— KATHARINE BUTLER HATHAWAY

Beyond the Mundane and Routine

Our ego mind prefers safety, routine, and the status quo. It does not want us to step too far out of the front door into anything too new or different. On the other hand, our essential self wants us to stretch, grow, shed what is unnecessary or heavy, and explore this life more fully.

A transition begins with an impulse from the soul to see new terrains and new horizons. We grow, become lighter, and see the world afresh by taking a step into the scary unknown. In a smooth transition, the desire to experience the adventure eventually outweighs the resistance, and thus the adventure begins. We leave behind an old life and move towards something new: we resign from the job to travel the world; we leave a long-standing stuck relationship and let our hair down and explore being on our own again; we move out of the city and experience living somewhere remote and different; we give up the 9 to 5 rat race and start our own business.

The impulse of the soul is always wanting to shake up our mundane routines and lead us forward on the path of passion and adventure. When we follow the adventure, then we feel happy, alive, and exhilarated. In my own life, I began to close down and seek safety after a difficult and incomplete transition from adolescent to young adult. Then in my twenties, I lived a fairly routine and shallow life, with no sense of adventure. My boat was parked firmly in a safe harbour, and I was not leaving, thank you very much.

When the impulse of the soul began to call me in my early thirties, at first I had no idea what was happening. Then the pain of staying in my safe harbour became too great, and I had to leave. Being out on the high sea felt scary and exhilarating. I had no idea where I was going; I just followed my heart and sailed by the north star. Naturally, my inner critic went crazy, as did other people around me. Others were just reflecting my own unresolved doubts and fears, and as I grew in confidence and certainty these outer reflections just faded away.

The inner critic likes to keep us in our familiarity zones. Whenever we get a little too bold or too big for our boots, our critic tells us to turn back, that it is dangerous to proceed, that we should hold onto what we already have, that we should not be frivolous or thoughtless, that we should put others before us, that we should not throw away our career or relationship, even though it keeps us miserable and playing small in life.

The inner critic is driven by our old conditioning. One of its prime directives is to keep us safe. Often, safety means conforming and not shining our light too brightly. Perhaps, the inner critic has us believe that we cannot trust anyone, not even ourselves. Usually, we expect the unknown will be worse than the known, even if our current reality is extremely painful. Fear takes many shapes and forms. We may fear the unknown, pain, defeat, or humiliation, what other people might think or say about us, or exile or rejection.

In a rough transition, the ego mind clamps down on the soul's impulse to grow, and this can lead to a more explosive and chaotic journey. In a smooth transition, the soul's impulse outweighs our resistance to take the first step. There is risk with every form of transition; there are no guarantees of the end result. Yet, in a smooth transition, usually we find our fears are not as big as we once thought.

At this point, it is worth mentioning an important distinction between stability and safety. This is something the resistant ego mind does not fully appreciate.

Stability is like the mountaineer who climbs a difficult path yet reaches his or her destination securely. Safety is the person who is too afraid or lacks any real motivation to begin that difficult path. Safety seeks guarantees before taking a single step out of the door.

On the other hand, stability plans for the journey as best as possible. With stability, there is the element of confidence and trust. We are confident in our own resilience and resourcefulness, and we trust in a higher power to guide us through. Safety is a denial of the heart and the dreams of the soul. The important thing to note if heading for a transition is that safety can work for a while, but in the long run it rarely turns out to be a meaningful or engaging strategy. I have met many people who put aside a gift or a dream in early life, out of doubt and fear, and then spend years in regret.

A transition is a process that has a beginning, a middle, and an end. The end is really a door to a whole new process and experience of life. A transition helps to complete one phase and open another. Whenever we follow our heart, we engage with a transition that is a journey into the unknown that brings us to a new horizon. When we leave the confining space of a tight familiarity zone and take off our ego-mind spectacles, we find there is a vaster and more intricate and intriguing world out there than we first realized. To find that world, we must take a step out of our tight familiarity zones.

12 REASONS TO FOLLOW OUR DREAMS

1. Every meaningful dream is a whisper from our highest future self speaking back to us down through time. There are important dreams and journeys that the soul wants us to actualize in divine timing. Every big dream holds the potential to align us with the resonance of our highest future.

2. Just playing with visualizing our dreams helps them feel closer, feel more alive, joyful, and excited. Thinking about our dreams is a great way to lift our energy and psychological state. In contrast, when we think constantly about problems and worst-case scenarios, we depress our energy and psychological state. Our dreams point to a more authentic and meaning-ful direction in life.

3. When we focus on our dreams, we start to stabilize the desired qualities and vibrations in our energy field. There are no limits to our ability to dream. Each dream we realize becomes a stepping stone for the next. When we don't dream we are suppressing our desires, and eventually we stop dreaming altogether. Then rather than possibility, we are allowing fear, guilt, or duty to define our life.

4. When we dream, we are telling our unconscious mind that this is what we want to invite into our lives. A dream connects us to the feeling we want, as well as to the experience. Our unconscious mind is a faithful servant, and it will start to organize our reality in line with our desires and expectations. Our unconscious mind is guided by the feeling we want to generate. A feeling of wanting more love, connection, joy, and exhilaration can be manifested in a thousand and one ways. We are not dependent on any one experience or situation.

5. When we follow a dream we start to engage more meaningfully with the life force. We discover and activate our inner potential through the journey. We awaken archetypal energies within us. We become more resourceful and capable as a result of the journey. Even when things do not turn out as expected, we grow in confidence through dealing with unexpected challenges.

6. By taking a step towards our heart's desire, we learn about confidence, courage, faith, freedom, and trust. On the journey, we learn that fear and excitement are two sides of the same coin.

7. When we choose a dream we also are choosing to let go and say no to anything not in line with this dream. We are freed, and others are also freed to pursue their highest path. There is nothing more exhilarating than breaking through our own sense of limitation and fear.

8. By activating a dream, we begin to synergize our left-brain intellect with right-brain imagination and intuition. The definition of synergy is that the sum of the whole is greater than the sum of the parts. We become more whole and real as a result of the journey.

9. In life, we pass through the stages of dependence and independence.

When we follow a heartfelt dream we learn about interdependence. This is about learning to co-create purposefully and meaningfully with others. Achieving a dream can lead to a rewriting of our inner life scripts.

10. Even when a dream does not work out exactly as intended (which is often the case), we learn through success and failure, which are merely two sides of the same coin. Both are forms of feedback that can lead to future goals and projects.

11. When we follow a dream, our Higher Self will begin to organize synchro-nicities and a set sequence of number of miracles so that the perfect people and situations are magnetized into our lives at the right time.

12. When we actualize a dream, we have something meaningful and real to share and offer to our loved ones. Our successes become an inspiration and resource for others on the path. There is probably no greater gift or legacy you can to leave your loved ones and descendants than actualizing your dreams and living a full and vital life.

With each little step you take into unknown territory, a pattern of strength develops. You begin feeling stronger and stronger and stronger.
— *SUSAN JEFFERS*

Transition Rewrites Our Life Scripts

Smooth transitions challenge us to find our own definition of the important things in life, such as contentment, happiness, and success. They also help us to navigate new landscapes where new rules of reality seem to apply. A transition also helps us to rewrite those rules from the inside out. The rules of reality can change when we change. I am not talking about the sun not rising in the morning; what I am talking about is how we attract more of the good things, such as wonder and delight, and repel the stuff that is not useful anymore, such as growing through suffering.

When Alice stepped into Wonderland, she had to learn a new set of games rules and apply them in a set of new situations. A smooth transition begins with a choice on some level, and a powerful choice can change everything. When we change, the world itself seems to change. When we take the journey, the old rules governing our reality start to wobble, shift, and change. A smooth transition can help us rewrite the hidden scripts of our lives.

When I grabbed the reins of my life in the early nineties, some 20 years ago, I resigned from a well-paid career in local government to follow my heart. This was a step of absolute courage and faith that seemed crazy to my rational mind. I had no idea where I was going; I only knew that I needed to take the journey. From the moment I resigned, I felt such an exhilarating sense of joy and aliveness in my body that it did not matter—I was feeling amazing. I had overcome my inner resistance to change and taken a gamble. Actually, gamble is not quite the right word, because I was very much in tune with my intuition and had the courage to follow it.

In hindsight, I know that it was the perfect moment to make the move. There were a number of synchronicities in the two years afterwards that moved me into the next phase of my working life. This was a time of tremendous creativity and innovation, intuition and play in my work. In this work, I got to hang out with many incredible authors, which set the scene for my later writing career. This, in turn, opened the door for my coaching and mentoring of authors and the writing retreats around the United Kingdom and Europe that followed. My zone around work and success expanded way beyond anything I had known up to that point.

This step of faith also put me in the perfect circumstances to meet my next partner. We spent an incredible 12 years together, and it was an experience of pure love. I had not experienced intimacy, love, and support to that degree before. Taking that one step all those years ago, and resigning from my well-paid but rather limiting job in local government, helped me rewrite the rules of my reality in ways I never could have dreamed possible back then. For many years, until my recent super-rough transition, the rules of reality seemed more fluid and positively malleable.

Deep within us there is a primordial knowledge or preconscious perception of our true nature, our destiny, our abilities and our calling in life. Not only do we have a particular path to follow but, on some instinctive level, we know what it is.

— *HOWARD SASPORTAS*

Transition, Direction, and Purpose

In his book *The Soul's Code*, psychologist James Hillman proposed that there is a calling in life somewhere inside us and that it's our lifelong mission to discover and act on that calling. He calls this the Acorn Theory and explains: 'Each life is formed by its unique image, an image that is the essence of that life and calls it to a destiny. As the force of fate, this image acts as a personal daemon, an accompanying guide who remembers your calling. The daemon motivates. It protects. It invents and persists with stubborn fidelity.'

This daemon is the way of purpose and our untapped potential. As James Hillman says, we have within us a purpose and a destiny that we may or may not realize. So many of us get caught up in mundane activities and forget the calling of the daemon. The daemon might be calling us to a more creative, dynamic, or adventurous life, but are we listening? Perhaps there is a dancer or a writer or a poet waiting to be liberated. Perhaps there is an adventurer or a magician or a teacher waiting to be activated in our lives.

Of course, we will never know unless we stop what we are currently doing, take the first step, and see what happens. Within us all are untapped qualities, skills, and abilities that we do not realize we have. These are sleeping seeds in the unconscious mind that remain sleeping unless we activate them. The journey, once accepted, is the activating force. Fear can very easily turn into excitement once we are on our way. Confusion and uncertainty can become clarity, as we take a few steps along the path.

Just by accepting the journey, our sense of self and possibility can begin to expand. We know we have taken a courageous step, and this allows other courageous steps to be taken more easily. Along the way, we hopefully learn that the journey is more important than the destination. The journey itself releases our inner potential. This is because our gifts and talents become tangible when we start using them. If we take the step, we find ourselves in a zone where we can experiment, play, and be more creative in our lives.

This is the path of mastery; there is no other way. The writer does not hone his or her skills by visualizing the work being done—the skills are awakened through the act of writing. This applies to any important area we want to open and develop. If we do not take the step into the unknown and follow a dream or a vision, our life always remains in the tight circle of the known.

> *You can trust the promise of this opening:*
> *Unfurl yourself into the grace of beginning*
> *This is at one with your life's desire.*
> — *JOHN O'DONOGHUE*

Transition Is About Limitless Possibility

A smooth transition is one way to experience the creative power of the light of the soul acting directly on the world. This opens new doors and possibilities in our outer reality. This is because the outer world is a reflection of our inner world. If we set positive intentions and focus on the end result we want, then this is what we will attract and create in our reality. Intentions are game changers: they can alter our core vibration. If we intend love, then we start to vibrate with love. If we intend ease and grace, then we start to vibrate with those qualities. Intention shifts our focus from problem to higher outcomes. If we focus on suffering, then this is what we will notice in the world. If we focus on opportunity and possibility, then this is what we will see in our experience. What we focus on we tend to attract and create. This is just one of the spiritual laws that govern this earthly plane.

Of course, I am not talking about ignoring the suffering in the world. There is a difference between having a grounded awareness and immersing oneself in the suffering of the world. It is important to have compassion and a broad awareness of what is going on in the world. It is also important to know that experience follows intention and focus. If we want to change our experience, then it behooves us to examine our intentions first. Most people have intentions that are either conflicting, confusing, or not very exciting. People with clear intentions have a clear focus and create clear results.

I met Asta some years ago. She went to America as an exchange student and fell in love with the country. She decided to go back, and two years later began a finance and business administration degree. When she completed the course, one of her professors recommended her for an internship where she earnt a 'ridiculous amount of money.' She did this for a time and then she decided she wanted to come back to Europe and arranged a transfer to Ireland. Despite being in a well-paid job and loving living in Ireland, she felt that something was missing. She quit and started doing random jobs that were mostly fun. Then she decided to go back to university.

'I found a course I wanted to do at a London university. I looked up the course, and I knew this is where I wanted to go. I was so sure. So I applied. The next thing I did was find the most beautiful image of the university library. I set that up as my desktop. I would sit down and think what it would be like if I was there in that library. I imagined the smell of books and the feel of holding them. I imagined walking up and down the staircase.

'Then I took a leap of faith, I decided to move to London ahead of hearing if I got accepted. I stayed in London with a friend for a few months. I was accepted, of course, and when I started the course I had the strong feeling that I belonged and this is what I was supposed to be doing. I completed a Master's degree in International Development.

'Not only was the experience amazing but I also began to see the world in a new way. I met people who were working with different organizations in the field, which was so fascinating. I felt a growing urge to be part of the change needed in the world. This led in time to my dream job, where I now travel the world and see places I would never have considered going. Not only that, this journey helped me change an old relationship that was not working. Now I live with an amazing man in the UK.'

I asked Asta what her biggest challenges on this journey were. She replied: 'I am an extrovert, and so I look for feedback; the challenge is to stick to what I believe is true without allowing other people's opinions to get in the way. Also, I was trained from a young age to be a harder worker. Now I have learnt to get energized by being in situations that come true because of my taking time to create them. I have learnt to keep focusing on the things that give me energy and inspiration.'

I then asked Asta what made the biggest difference for her in stepping onto this path, and she said: 'The biggest difference came from an inner sense of force—knowing what I want and the sense that I can have it. What I mean by this is not a loud force but a quiet internal force. Also I have found that writing down my dreams or somehow externalizing it in some other way is very helpful. I need to move it from just thoughts inside my head to something I can see on paper or a computer screen or on a vision board. This helps me imagine what it is like to have wild success.'

The two most important requirements for major success are: first, being in the right place at the right time, and second, doing something about it.

— *RAY KROC*

Transition and Perfect Timing

With every transition, there is certainly a question of right timing. Often, we need to learn patience and trust around making the right choice at the right time. Sometimes, we delay making the right choice because of unprocessed doubts and fears. This is fine so long as we do the work and do not delay too long.

A decade ago, Samantha had a dream of going to New Zealand, but also she had a lot of fears and doubts about the decision. Others close to her also painfully reflected back these fears and doubts. I helped her to work through her resistance to connect with her heart and the dream that was alive within her. After a year or so, she followed her heart.

Some years later, we spoke about her experience of following a meaningful dream. 'Moving to Auckland was really very exciting. I came on holiday here some time before thinking about my move, and I remember it felt just like home. At that time I had a real heart experience, and I fell in love with the country. I had travelled lots before and never had a similar feeling. The inner journeys I did with Steve helped me to get clear that this was the right decision. It helped me see and neutralize the negative influence of some people around me who did not agree with my decision.

'On the plane to New Zealand I felt excited, and free. I spent six weeks in Thailand on the way. When I arrived things, there were challenges. But I have been here now for six years, and so much has happened in that time. I have explored much of this beautiful landscape, and I have my own business, which I love. Above all, this decision has led me not only into a brilliant adventure but it has also led me to feel happier and more confident in myself. I definitely now feel more me and happy to be me.'

The soul has important dreams that come to fruition in perfect timing. I had not seen Clare for several months, then we made contact and arranged to meet for tea in a tea shop in Stoke Newington. As we were drinking our tea, she smiled and told me she had some news. She was expecting a baby and was three months pregnant. I knew she had been trying with her partner for nearly four years and had almost given up hope that it would happen.

She continued to drink her tea and she told me the story.

'The harder I tried the more things did not work; bringing pressure to it did not help. Then, when I found out, I was completely elated. By the second week there was a complication, and I was bleeding all week and was afraid I would lose the baby. But everything is now alright. I do not know that it has sunk in that it is real. Then again, at another level, I feel a whole octave shift. What I mean is that what it feels like to be Clare has shifted. A whole piece of my neurotic patterning has been taken out. I tend to be an anxious person. Now, I have no worry.

'Having the baby is a great leap of faith. After finding out I was pregnant, I let go of my consultancy role after eight years of working for the company. On the one hand, this was a great relief, and on the other, there is of course the need to pay the bills. My partner is also possibly going to be made redundant around the time the baby is due. How we are going to manage we do not know, but we both have this absolute sense of trust. It is so mysterious and it feels really right.'

NURTURE YOUR DREAMS

Write down your responses to the following questions.

1. What do you love doing now? What makes you feel good now? What makes your spirit dance and sing now?
2. What activities bore you or deaden you or irritate you or stress you? Then note down how much time per day or each week you devote to these activities.
3. What dreams do you have that you would love to realize? What secret ambitions, large or small, do you have? What skills or qualities would you love to develop? What experiences would you like to have? What feelings do you want to experience? What is your ideal way of living in the world?
4. If you were to have one wild impossible dream, what would that be? How important is this dream? How excited do you feel about it when you visualize yourself achieving your highest outcome in this area of your life?
5. Now review everything you have written. Notice if anything jumps out of the page or surprises you. What are you going to do now that is different as a result?

DWELL UPON HIGHEST
POSSIBLE OUTCOMES

1. This is about contemplating your highest possible outcomes and wildest dreams. There is no reason to sell yourself short. Aim high, and be open to new, expansive experiences of what you want to attract or create in your life.

2. Contemplate what you want to attract or create in positive terms. Your unconscious mind does not understand a negative. What this means is, do not think of a pink flamingo floating through the room now, because by doing so your unconscious mind simply creates the image of a pink flamingo floating through the room.

3. Describe your positive outcome or dream in sensory-based language, meaning describe what you would see, hear, touch, and smell when you experience this realized dream.

4. Imagine describing your dream in terms of the when, the where, the how, and with whom you will create this dream outcome.

5. Imagine turning your dream outcome inside your imagination into a short video film. Imagine that you are in a cinema watching the film and yourself as an actor in this film. After a few minutes, imagine stepping into the film and experiencing the dream as if it is happening around you.

Keep a Smooth Transitions Journal

One way to keep track of your adventure is to keep a journal. Journaling can also help you clarify your thoughts, feelings, needs, desires, and expectations. It also gives your unconscious mind the message that your journey is important. Keep your journal with you at all times to jot down any ideas and thoughts related to your passions, goals, visions, and dreams.

Here, you can write about: What you think and imagine yourself doing, what interests and excites you, when you feel the most passionate, conversations that inspire you, a book or film that moved you, a person or people you love being around, people who support you emotionally, a space that make you feel creative or open or grateful, and when you feel most in your flow. You can also write about the challenges of the journey and your feelings about navigating those challenges.

Take time (evenings are often best) to read and reflect on the entries in your journal. This will help to keep the momentum of inspiration, desire, and expectation high.

4

Rough Transitions

In Yann Martel's novel, *Life of Pi*, Pi is a boy who has grown up in Pondicherry, India, where his family runs a zoo. When he is 16, his father decides to close the family business and move his family to Canada. They book passage with their animals on a Japanese freighter. One night, there is a heavy storm, and while Pi is on deck the boat hits problems. He rushes down to find his family, but he cannot reach them. A crew member throws him into a lifeboat, and he watches helplessly as the ship sinks, killing his family and all its crew.

Although no-one survives, a few animals manage to climb aboard the lifeboat. After the storm, Pi finds himself in the company of an injured zebra, an orangutan, and a spotted hyena. He watches helplessly as the hyena kills the zebra and also mortally wounds the orangutan. Suddenly, a tiger emerges from under the tarp and kills and eats the hyena. Pi is now adrift in the middle of the Pacific Ocean in a small boat with a ferocious hungry tiger.

● ● ●

In life, there is the rough and the smooth. Obviously, most of us would prefer the smooth, but there are times when only a rough transition will do the job. A rough transition involves considerable challenge. Whether that experience of challenge is joyful or involves suffering is up to us. If we respond more to pain, then the soul will utilize a rough transition. Of course, some people really relish a challenge and can rise to the occasion more than others—they can handle crisis and chaos better than others. But even the strongest amongst us can find a rough transition to be sudden, fierce, and unpredictable. It can feel like being caught in a raging storm, or even being shipwrecked. The latter is what I would call a super-rough transition. This involves quite a different degree of challenge, because it offers an opportunity for rapid spiritual awakening and growth.

A super-rough transition can feel like Pi in the story—stranded in a lifeboat the middle of an expansive ocean with no food or drinking water and a hungry tiger as a companion. Here, we face an existential crisis of some kind. We feel adrift in a vast ocean, with no clear sense of direction or meaning. Our life may feel in danger of collapse. The soul wants us to grow and wake up from the illusions of this world and will use whatever means it can to achieve this end.

This is a risky path, because there are no guarantees that we will make it to the other side. We will encounter suffering in ourselves, and the danger is that suffering can have a destructive psychical and psychological impact; we can get caught up in it. The soul chooses this path because it offers a fast track to personal growth and spiritual awakening. If we embrace the suffering rather than fight it, then we have a greater chance of making it through intact.

I need to say upfront that a transition is not about divine punishment, for such a thing does not exist. We live in a lawful universe, and I am not talking about societal laws. Every thought, choice, word uttered, and action has consequences. There are consequences that feel pleasant and others that do not. This is the principle of karma. We reap what we sow. The soul grows through experiencing both the light and the dark.

A super-rough transition can feel like a passage through darkness. In the dark, we can learn and grow. In the dark passage, some lessons and experiences break open our ego defences and reveal our as-yet-unknown potential, and thus move us in a new direction. Even so, when we are caught up in a rough or super-rough storm, it is wise to remember the old prayer, "God grant me the serenity to accept the things that cannot be changed, courage to change the things I can, and the wisdom to know the difference."

The Adventure Begins

Paul had a painful story to share. 'Everything went when Ann died,' Paul told me. They had lived together for 15 years when Ann started to feel ill. Then one day, Paul came home to find Ann collapsed on the floor. She died in hospital shortly afterwards, of lung cancer. In accordance with her wishes, she was cremated and her ashes taken out to sea and scattered off the coast of Ireland. Paul told me that he staggered through life in the months that followed.

He went to see a bereavement counsellor, who helped a little, but the one thing that made him forget was throwing himself into his work. Paul worked in construction, mainly on roofs. Around nine months after Ann's death, he had pushed himself so hard that on one fateful occasion he slipped and fell through a roof. He severely damaged his back, which left him in hospital for 14 months. He was forced to give up his line of work and just wait for his health to recover. After the loss of Ann and his accident, he was plunged headlong into a rough transition.

We can grow through stepping towards our dreams, and we can also grow through chaos, crisis, and confusion; no path is better than another. When all movement or hope is blocked, a rough or super-rough transition is often the soul's response. Perhaps, we find ourselves in a loveless marriage or a dull job and pretend that everything is alright, but deep down we know everything is far from alright.

In such circumstances, things often come to a head during a powerful astrological transit, such as a Saturn Return at the age of 28 or a Chiron Return at the age of 50. At such times, the safe boat of our life suddenly hits choppy waters. If we ignore the signs, we then head straight into a raging storm. Whenever a difficult transition happens, there is at first shock and disbelief—and then feelings of why me? why this? why now?

I know that during my own experience of a rough transition, I felt all these things. It was like life had suddenly dealt me a bad set of cards and I was the innocent party in the whole affair. How could spirit do this to me? Confusion, indignation, and anger soon followed. Then hot on their heels was raw grief. Everything I had learnt about accepting responsibility for the reality I was creating went out of the window. Surely, I was not creating all this? But deep down I knew that I was not a victim of circumstance; I was an active player in the drama.

At the time, the experience felt too harsh and raw for me to completely accept my part in setting it up. In hindsight, I now realize that even though my life then was happy, I had stopped living life as a magical adventure. One of my beliefs about life is that we are here to have fun and celebrate the life force. We are also here to stretch, grow, and realize the fullness of who we are; we are not here to have fun at the expense of growth. This is not really fun but an avoidance of who we truly are at the centre of our being. When we have stopped living the adventure of life, then we enter the zone where a rough transition is one option to move us back on the path again. Sometimes, a transition turns into an existential crisis, which is a super-rough transition.

Elizabeth Lesser wrote about her own existential crisis in her moving book, *Broken Open*. Her essential message is that positive life change can emerge from life-altering events. Elizabeth Lesser comments: 'How strange that the nature of life is change, yet the nature of human beings is to resist change. And how ironic that the difficult times we fear might ruin us are the very ones that can break us open and helps us blossom into who we were meant to be.'

In the book, Elizabeth talks about a trip to Jerusalem. One morning, she walked through the streets, with their mosques, temples, churches, and markets, and wandered deeper into the walled city. There, she came across an ancient alleyway lined with shops selling religious artefacts. One shop appealed to her, and she went in. On the floor was a patchwork of rugs, and on the walls hung small paintings of different saints. She saw in a back room two Arab men drinking tea. One was older than the other, and the younger man stepped out of the back room, greeted Elizabeth, and took her hand and led her towards the older man.

'The old man stood and shuffled over to greet me. He placed his right hand on his heart and bowed his head in traditional Islamic greeting.' The man pointed at a small painting hanging on the wall, with an inscription that read 'AND THE TIME CAME WHEN THE RISK TO REMAIN TIGHT IN A BUD WAS MORE PAINFUL THAN THE RISK IT TOOK TO BLOSSOM.'

Unexpected tears stung her eyes, and she turned away. The men asked what was wrong, and she replied nothing was wrong. The older man persisted, saying, 'Something is wrong. You are in pain … because you are afraid … afraid of yourself.' Elizabeth was heading for a transition. Sometime later, she entered into a love affair with a man she called her 'shaman lover.' The affair lasted a year and eventually led to the breakdown of her marriage.

When I interviewed Elizabeth for a podcast, she told me: 'My self-image as a good mother, a good wife, a good person was really shattered when my marriage crumbled. I never thought it would happen to me; no one in my family had ever gone through it. It made me feel like there was something profoundly wrong about me, and it sent me spiralling down into a place in which I started to feel I was losing everything.'

Her life had plunged into deceit, infidelity, and darkness, but along the way her heart cracked open, and she emerged in her own words as more alive, passionate, and real.

Most people live, whether physically, intellectually or morally,
in a very restricted circle of their potential being.

— *WILLIAM JAMES*

The Adventure Can Be Refused

As we approach a rough or super-rough transition, we usually have little conscious idea of what is happening. Everything is being set up at a soul level. Yet deep down our body, or unconscious intelligence, is aware that something is happening. Because we are not so in touch with our body intelligence, intuition, and feelings, we keep on going regardless. We pretend everything is alright and carry on as normal. Perhaps we feel an 'odd' feeling and try to make it go away.

We might change our diet, go to the gym more often, get a new girlfriend or boyfriend, do some retail therapy

But nothing much really shifts. We are moving the furniture of our lives rather than moving home. We are living on the surface of our lives, rather than diving into the fast flowing river of life. By doing so, we are refusing the journey and remain stuck.

The good news is the refusal does not stop the journey. The forces acting upon our lives are too strong, and we cannot resist the oncoming shift. This shift can so easily become a crisis. A redundancy comes out of the blue, our health takes a turn for the worse, our partner walks out and leaves us. There are a thousand ways a crisis can be triggered. When it happens, we have reached the point of no return, a rough transition has been initiated, and we are on our way.

Sometimes, we choose a hard route because the pain and intensity of the experience helps to break through many ego barriers to our life force and soul calling. A hard route can help break through external barriers, such as a rigid, unsupportive family. It can move us to leave oppressive cultural norms and seek out a new life. Life is not always about sailing through calm seas. Storms are often necessary, because they are challenging, cleansing, and invigorating. Carl Jung once said, 'There is no coming to consciousness without pain.' Yet storms are also painful, and this is something to be aware of. Pain can indicate a cleansing is going on. Pain can be necessary for our spiritual health, even though this is not easy.

Matthew Fox, the author of *Original Blessing*, states: 'Facing the darkness, admitting the pain, allowing the pain to be pain, is never easy. This is why courage—big-heartedness—is the most essential virtue on the spiritual journey. But if we fail to let pain be pain … then pain will haunt us in nightmarish ways. We will become pain's victims instead of the healers we might become.'

In a rough or super-rough transition, the calling to adventure means facing pain. It means going from the known to the unknown. We do not like pain, and we are encouraged to suppress pain with drugs. This is why refusing the calling is so common. There are many great mythological stories that deal with a central character refusing a calling and then suffering the consequences or struggling to rectify the mistake.

In *Star Wars*, Luke Skywalker initially turns down the opportunity to fly off his planet with Obi Wan and the two droids—he has too many responsibilities, and his aunt and uncle need him. In the Biblical story of Jonah and the whale, Jonah the prophet was ordered by God to go to the city of Nineveh and to preach against their wicked ways. Instead of obeying this command, Jonah ran in the opposite direction and took a ship to the city of Tarshish. But a great storm arose, and when the finger of blame pointed to Jonah, he was thrown overboard and swallowed by a great fish that took him to the city of Tarshish.

We may be afraid of unknown dangers or shrink at the thought of undertaking a journey that involves any element of loss or risk. The adventure doesn't just go away because we reject it; it becomes a source of pain, reminding us of our weakness, fears, and frustration. Joseph Campbell says: 'Refusal of the summons converts the adventure into its negative. Walled-in boredom, hard work, or "culture," the subject loses the power of significant affirmative action and becomes a victim to be saved.'

We may refuse the journey for a time, but eventually we may find ourselves pulled along anyway. The soul will have its way with us. When we refuse the journey, then we will resist. Resistance can evoke strong emotions. How we deal with these emotions is a crucial factor on the journey.

Adventure and the Emotional Abyss

In Buddhism, and particularly in Zen, the lotus flower is a common symbol for awakening and enlightenment. The roots of a lotus go deep into the mud, silt, and debris, and from this it grows through the water and emerges into the bright sunlight as a beautiful, fragrant flower. The lotus does not grow in a pure, rarefied atmosphere; it grows from decayed matter.

When we are pulled into an unwelcome adventure, then we enter an emotional roller-coaster. We are unprepared for such a journey, and it can trigger unresolved issues in the emotional energy field. Some of these are from childhood, where we felt rejected, invisible, too visible, or not loved enough. Perhaps, we have unresolved issues from our adolescence. Here, emotion and sexual energy can intertwine and get stuck. Perhaps, we had our heart broken. Perhaps, we lost our sense of self and our way through the world.

When the transition begins, we are sent tumbling down into the emotional abyss, where live the hungry ghosts of anxiety, chaos, depression, fear, grief, guilt, regret, and toxic shame. When these arise, dealing with everyday reality becomes more challenging. We cannot see the world clearly. We are feeling old emotional responses along with reactions to the current transition. This is very confusing.

Emotional overwhelm can lead us to become more reactive. Being reactive, we can get ourselves into situations that demand even more energy than we have to give. Being reactive tends to push people away who could be helpful in some way. Being reactive creates more inner turbulence. Emotions are energy in motion:

they are meant to flow like storm clouds or waterfalls. When our emotional energy becomes trapped in repetitive destructive patterns, then we suffer.

I met Gerri in Greece, in the summer of 2012. She shared her story in a healing circle. She had been married for nearly three years. Her husband had bipolar disorder. She knew this when she married him. One day he took off, and when he came back, he confessed that he had slept with another woman and that the woman was pregnant. Confused and not knowing what to do, she left her home town of New Orleans to clear her head and gain some clarity. I sat and listened to her relate this experience through many tears, with her saying: 'Should I stay or should I go? I just do not know what to do.'

A traumatic experience can create a great surge of emotions that need time to process and integrate. Liz was thrust into a rough transition when her best friend unexpectedly died in an accident in India. She fell and hit her head and went into a coma, and three days later she passed over.

Liz says of this time: 'My emotional journey was indescribable. It was so heartbreaking. I went through a lot of heartache, as if my heart was being broken in the most painful way. I did not know how to help myself; I did not know what sort of help I really needed. I thought I would be alright if everyone would go away and leave me alone. I had the thought that despite doing so much personal development and spiritual work I should have managed better. I did not know how to be gentle with myself. I did not know how to love myself. It has been a journey of learning about my boundaries, learning to say no without feeling guilty.

'Some people may have thought I was being selfish, but I was learning to take care of myself. I thought the cathartic was what I needed to do. Now I know that my nervous system cannot cope with prolonged catharsis. I was also going numb. I just froze in shock and did not start thawing out until several months later. When I did, it felt that tension was leaving my body giving more space to my emotions of grief and I started to feel again. Lots of moments where I did not believe she was gone; it just did not make sense. I have had beautiful moments of her holding me in lucid dreams and in waking moments, in my frozen moments I found everything quite overwhelming. For many months I was just angry and irritable.'

The emotional abyss is a difficult part of the journey. Anger, guilt, hurt, confusion, and shock are all part of the mix. (Please note: when I talk about shock, I am not talking about clinical shock, which can lead to collapse, coma, or death; I am talking about a wider definition of shock, which includes a wide range of symptoms, such as panic attacks, depression, numbness, disorientation, and disassociation.) Shock is a sign that something is still being processed in the bodymind system.

Confusion comes when we leave the familiarity of our old life and begin to enter something radically new and different. Confusion is natural when our reality begins to shift. That being said, there are layers to shock, and they may not all clear until the transition has fully passed.

Another emotion that can arise is guilt, which can be a tricky emotion to deal with. It arises with the conviction that something has been done that should not have been done. Perhaps a moral code, value, or belief has been compromised. Guilt is linked to deep loyalty to our family. We can feel guilty for rocking the boat, not being perfect or good enough, or speaking openly about an area that is deemed taboo by our family.

Of course, guilt might be a sign that we need to release something that never truly belonged to us in the first place. Alice Miller once wisely said, 'Many people suffer all their lives from this oppressive feeling of guilt, the sense of not having lived up to their parents' expectations ... no argument can overcome these guilt feelings, for they have their beginnings in life's earliest period, and from that they derive their intensity.' We may feel guilty because in some way we have instigated the transition or encouraged it or yielded to it and this causes self-judgement and self-blame. Guilt is paralyzing, and if not checked can lead to shame and depression.

Another common emotion we often meet here is anger. Anger is a powerful emotion, and it is never a good idea to try and suppress it. Anger can be expressed in either a healthy or destructive way. If we have grown up to fear other people's anger we may fear our own. Perhaps we learnt that our own anger was unhealthy. Anger can be a healthy and cleansing emotion when it is positively expressed. Healthy or clean anger is non-judgemental and does not attack another or self; rather, it just states a perspective and sets a boundary. Unhealthy anger conveys the message that another person is to blame for our situation. Expressing clean anger takes us higher up the emotional scale and is a force for liberation and positive change. Another difficult emotion for many people is grief. In my own recent experience of transition, this was one of the most difficult feelings I had to process. Transition brings loss and the end of a phase of life. The more significant the loss, the more intense the grief tends to be. Grief is inevitable, and grieving is a personal and highly individual experience. How you move through grief depends on various factors, such as your coping style, your life experience, your faith, and the intensity and nature of the loss.

There are different unhelpful myths about grief. These include the myths that pain will go away if you ignore it; it is important to always be strong in the face of grief; and crying is the only appropriate way to grieve. I would say that there is no set time to heal grief, and the process should not be rushed. Even after dealing with strong grief in my transition, it continued for some years in my dreams.

Grief is an appropriate response to the loss of a friend, relationship, or phase of life. Grief can be silent or loud. Tears are healing, and it is always appropriate to cry in order to let go of something or someone. C. S. Lewis married late in life and enjoyed a deeply fulfilling relationship before his wife Joy died of cancer. He wrote: 'Grief turns out to be a place none of us know until we reach it. We anticipate (we know) that someone close to us could die, but we do not look beyond the few days or weeks that immediately follow such an imagined death.'

The sum total of all these emotions can be overwhelming if many emotions are triggered at once. It can be hard to unpick them all and know what is going on, because it feels too overwhelming. If this was not enough in the emotional abyss, we may find other buried emotions being triggered that have nothing to do with the current experience but are more about our earlier years. This, in effect, leads to a kind of emotional double-whammy. There is also the triple-whammy, where you are also dealing with the emotional turbulence of other people who have views, opinions, and judgements about your transition.

In a super-rough transition, this journey can turn into a dark night of the soul. The emotional roller-coaster becomes a space that is dark and hopeless. There are few words that can really describe this space. I once met a man who was bitten by a poisonous spider in India, which threw his whole life into chaos. His body could no longer tolerate certain foods, and he became emotionally very sensitive. There is no two ways about it: navigating the emotional abyss is a challenging time.

THE EMOTIONAL ABYSS

BIG PICTURE — Avoid getting bogged down in too much bitty detail. Develop a sense of perspective, and stay focused on the bigger picture. At the very least, the bigger picture is making it through to the other side. Keeping an eye on the bigger picture, then prioritize important tasks and tackle them one at a time.

FEELINGS – Embrace all of the pain, grief, and anger that arises in you. Witness everything, and do not deny any difficult feelings. Avoid expressing these feelings in any hurtful ways to another person. Accept your life is changing, and that all uncertainty, confusion, or anxiety will pass.

HAVE COMPASSION – Others may judge you or be angry with you. Avoid reacting, and take time to pause and reflect before responding to the emotionally charged communications of other people. Practise lovingkindness as far as you can.

PATIENCE – When you feel overwhelmed by emotion, take your time and do not rush into making any decision or into taking action. Reflect long before you speak or act.

PHYSICAL BODY – Stay present to your body. Practise being aware of the natural cycle of your breath throughout the day—this will help you stay more mindful, calm, and present.

STRESS – Watch out for any warning signs of fatigue or burnout. Consider doing activities in short sharp bursts rather than keeping on going. Take time to rest and recuperate. A rough transition can leave you with a strong sense of stress or shock that needs time to heal.

SUPPORT – Remember that you do not have to struggle with problems on your own. Talking things through with someone you trust can often help to maintain a brighter outlook. Build a network of trusted people whose opinions you value, who can offer you different kinds of help and support. Remember to use prayer and meditation to ask your Higher Self and guides for support and healing.

VIBRATIONAL MEDICINE – Vibrational medicine offers simple and effective help for stress and shock. The most useful Bach Flower remedies to use in a tough transition are: Star of Bethlehem for grief, sadness, and shock; Mustard for deep gloom; Olive for mental exhaustion and trauma; Rock Rose for panic; and Sweet Chestnut for extreme mental anguish. If uncertain, use Rescue Remedy, which contains a blend of the most potent flower remedies.

Yes, perhaps we needed that dark winter.
Perhaps our dormancy was part of the plan –
For lifetimes, even aeons to ponder
Our heart's desires and whether God
Favours love and freedom,
Or erects prison bars?

— *GILL EDWARDS*

Navigating a Rough Passage

Rough transitions take us on a difficult journey that potentially leads us into a whole new phase of life. Our old life has been shipwrecked, and we have been left bereft on the rocks. A crisis can throw us off kilter. We lose balance, and we lose our way. We may even go numb for a time. Rough transitions are a kind of do-or-die thing; they force us to dive deep to find the strength and qualities to complete the course.

I met Susie at a workshop, and later through a friend, and instantly liked her. I did not know when we first met that she had gone through a powerful, tough transition.

She told me: 'When my marriage broke down, in 2009, I was so unhappy. I was a solicitor, a mortgage on two properties, and on the face of it I had it all, but I felt trapped. Then one day, when I was at the kitchen sink, washing up, I just felt depressed. It was then I started therapy, which taught me tools to trust my instincts and to honour my boundaries.

'Nine months later, I was diagnosed with breast cancer, and my doctors recommended chemo and wanted to take my breast off. I instinctively felt this was not right, and I decided to take matters into my own hands. I went and took some advice, changed my diet drastically, and started an exercise regime that included supplements. I took time off work, which gave me the opportunity to look into the illness and myself. I discovered after much self-inquiry that my illness was about learning to love myself. It was teaching me I did not have time to waste or bullshit anymore.'

I know many people who have gone through tough experiences and who state that they were changed for the better. For instance, I have heard people say that their cancer was the best thing that happened to them.

One man lost all his money. He had part owned a financial services company and was quite successful. One day, he woke up to find that his business partners had cheated him out of $750 million. To make matters worse, his wife, upon learning of this, became very angry and left him, taking their two children. After a couple of turbulent months, he came to realize that it was one of the best things that had ever happened to him. He had let go of two fraudulent business partners, plus an unhappy marriage. Soon afterwards, he came up with an idea for a new business that proved to be even more profitable, less stressful, and more enjoyable than his previous business.

Immaculee Ilibagiza grew up in Rwanda, which was ripped apart in 1994, as the country descended into a bloody genocide. Immaculee's family was brutally murdered, but incredibly, Immaculee survived the slaughter. For 91 days, she and seven other women huddled silently together in the cramped bathroom of the home of a local pastor while hundreds of armed men hunted for them. It was during those endless hours waiting in that cramped room that Immaculee discovered the power of prayer, forgiveness, and unconditional love. This was so strong in her that she was able to seek out and forgive her family's killers. I met her several years ago, at a talk in London, whilst she was promoting a book about her experiences called *Left to Tell*. She is a shining example of someone who has gone through a harrowing experience and come out a 'better' person on the other side.

In a super-rough transition, we can face a 'dark night of the soul' experience. Here, we lose all sense of meaning, belonging, and direction in the world. This is an extremely difficult journey, in which we face our darkness before we wake up to our light. Sita experienced a super-rough transition after a kundalini awakening that was triggered by intense spiritual practice. This led to anxiety and confusion, as her life started to unravel. She lost all sense of meaning and direction in life.

A super-rough transition can lead to shock and confusion and the feeling that everything is falling apart. This is the way of the mythic descent into the underworld. The underworld journey can be intense and destabilizing, and it requires tremendous courage and endurance. Here, all connection to the soul and Higher Self are severed. We find ourselves moving alone in the dark. and we may face many inner demons.

We have to walk in the faith that we are not abandoned. The passage seems to be never-ending. Guidance or mentoring by someone who knows the way can be invaluable. Unfortunately, few people who have made the passage have made sense of the experience. This is one of the reasons why I have written this book. I believe many people will follow in my footsteps in the coming decades and find themselves lost in a dark labyrinth with no-one around who really understands what is happening.

The good news to always bear in mind is that if you find yourself here, you are in a process. Even though it feels extremely challenging, there is light at the end of the tunnel. You may not see or feel that light for a period of time. But the light is always there, waiting for your emergence.

> *Don't worry that your life is turning upside down.*
> *How do you know that the side you are used to is better*
> *than the one to come?*
>
> — *RUMI*

Gifts of a Rough Passage

As we pass through a transition, we begin to access a more healthy emotional space, where we access higher octaves of forgiveness, compassion, self-love, and inner tranquillity. This may take weeks, months, or years, depending on the severity of the journey. A simple rule of thumb is, the more difficult the journey the more potential there is for total transformation. Also, the more we can trust a higher power, the less likely we will react and create unnecessary diversions along the way. If we complete the journey, then we can be purged of restrictive or toxic situations. The journey forces us to release people and situations that no longer serve our inner light. This is not about throwing the past away; it is about honouring the past, extracting the learning, and releasing others to their own highest path.

The more we can release what does not serve us, the easier it will be to shift our core vibration. We are no longer carrying the weight or burden of heavy situations. We can let go and let God, so to speak. We can release toxic fear and self-doubt, and this allows us to access higher octaves of joy and love. This grants us a certain freedom of thought and movement in the world. Furthermore, jettisoning the old life allows a new one to enter.

Here, we can find a growing yearning to find our true soul tribe. This is what the Irish call *anam caras*, or 'soul friends,' the ones who come to help and challenge us on our journey. As we shift, our task is to bring our lives more into balance. Our ability to manifest our highest path gets stronger. We are less subject to forces of collective consciousness that do not understand spiritual laws. We become more resourceful. We become more confident in our abilities to get through anything life throws at us. In time, we can step onto a new life trajectory, one we would never have found under our own steam alone.

This is essentially about life purpose—we discover why we are here. This discovery often comes in layers or steps. The next step is revealed, and only after we have taken it will further steps be shown to us. This is not to say there is only one way forward. Some paths are quicker than others. Some paths offer more opening than others. Passing through a storm is one way to powerfully activate inner dormant soul qualities or abilities. There is a great sense of urgency to dig deep within and find a solution or alternate way forward.

Sometimes, the severity of the journey is needed to shake loose some inner quality or qualities from the bedrock of the psyche. As they rise to the surface of consciousness, they begin to become more active in our lives. Intuition may become sharper as a result of a transition. Other gifts may also arise, such as a courage we never knew we possessed. We start to become the hero in our own play. We may feel a sudden and surprising surge of creative energy, which can manifest as a set of sculptures or paintings, or just as easily, a new business or a new child. We may feel a desire to play more and have fun, which can be especially liberating if life was too serious and left-brained. Perhaps more specific abilities arise, such as an ability to envision a project or lead a group of people. There can be a spiritual shift, allowing for a surge of love and compassion for others or the world itself. The list is endless.

Most importantly, with the big shifts comes a shift in identity. We do not see ourselves in the same way. Sometimes, this shift is not recognized straight away by others. It might even confuse some people. This can be the case in a relationship when one person suddenly shifts, leaving the other person confused. Sometimes, this results in a breakup. A shift in identity can affect many areas of life. For instance, before my recent transition I never really saw myself as a writer. I had written two books but saw it more as a hobby or something I wanted to experience than a serious pursuit. During and after my transition, this all changed. Now, writing is at the very centre of my life.

Some transitions come to wake us up completely. Here, our nervous system is flooded with increasing light. This is not easy in the early stages, but as we stabilize we have more access to the realm of soul. We can access timelines within the soul, and we may dream of other aspects of ourselves exploring other dimensions. We may have a desire to simplify our lives, to enjoy being in the moment more. For some, it can feel like Neo in *The Matrix*—suddenly waking up to see a new reality, able to see through the limited and highly repetitive patterns that keep humanity in unnecessary struggle and conflict. Such an awakening takes time and patience to integrate. Afterwards, there is nothing to do, and paradoxically, there comes a desire to serve in some way. In time, this can convert into a path of meaningful action, perhaps finding a worthy cause to join or initiating something very new.

GIFTS OF A ROUGH OR SUPER-ROUGH TRANSITION

AWAKENING – A spiritual transition can clear inner pathways and allow for a greater connection to soul and spirit. Our gut feeling and intuition becomes much sharper. Our sense of trust in the Universe increases, and we open to synchronicity, miracles, and flow. We become beacons of light in the world to help in the great global transition happening now.

FORGIVENESS – A spiritual transition helps us forgive ourselves and others. To forgive the past is a blessing. We all make mistakes, and no-one is perfect. At a deeper level, we have invited the transition to come in and no-one is to blame, especially ourselves.

HEALING – A transition can clear old emotional wounds and patterns and allow us to experience a new space. Perhaps, we have to face old core fears, and in the facing we clear the pattern. Healing can come in many ways. Sometimes, a transition may shift a painful family pattern. Perhaps a relationship is healed in some way as the light flows into the situation.

IDENTITY – A big transition helps to shift our sense of self. We take off limiting labels and judgements in order to adopt a broader and truer sense of self. We see ourselves in new ways, and this opens us up to new experiences. This can include feeling into our spiritual identity and seeing ourselves as more than an ego with a body. This is where our identity can become as vast and mysterious as the universe itself.

LOVE – A spiritual transition helps us redefine our relationships, and in time our own relationship, with love. Love is the ultimate reality, but we are often caught up in ego dramas around love. A rough transition can show us our core patterns around love and relating and help us move to a new level of experience around love.

MANIFESTATION – We create our reality. We also co-create our reality with our Higher Self and Sacred Unity. During a transition, our ability to manifest our path may feel severely hampered. This is how it should be, since our ego-self may wish to create something to avoid the transition process. A transition, once complete, increases our manifesting potential.

PURPOSE – A spiritual transition clears the decks for our latent dreams to become clearer. Our values and priorities may shift, which leads to a change in direction. Perhaps, chasing money becomes a lower priority than family, or vice-versa, with a career suddenly becoming more important than family.

RELEASE – A spiritual transition shakes much from our life, and we are emptied of anything tying us down to an old stage of life. We might not like this very much, and it probably will bring up grief and other emotions. But further down the line, we may feel grateful that so much flotsam and jetsam have been released to allow in the new.

RESOURCES – A spiritual transition brings us face to face with new situations, new people, and eventually, new opportunities. A tough transition will demand resources from you that you did not know you possessed. It will take you on a journey you did not know was possible for you to make.

RESONANCE – A spiritual transition confronts us with our core resistance to life—our confusion, doubt, and fear. We discover they have less power to influence us. Our resonance shifts up the vibrational scale, and we feel more connection to higher levels of compassion, love, inner peace, and purpose.

SERVICE – When we find ourselves on the other side of a transition, the concept of service often becomes an important one. We feel the soul moving in our lives, and we realize the paradox that all life is sacred and at the same time all life is impermanent. We are here to serve the life force. There are many ways to do this. Silent communion with the Higher Self is important. Also being in the world and exploring different ways to serve.

SOUL GIFTS – A spiritual transition awakens our gifts and talents. A transition is a fast learning track. If you have come to awaken your Inner Healer, you may suddenly face a challenge that requires you to heal yourself, a situation, or another. If you have come to awaken the Hero, then you may be flung into an immediate challenge that requires all your courage.

SYNERGY – A spiritual transition can address certain imbalances in our life. If we live too much in our heads, then a transition can bring us back to our heart. If we are too left or right brained. then it will seek to activate the less active side and create instead a more synergistic partnership between both.

TRANSFORMATION – A spiritual transition brings more consciousness into our lives. Unconscious patterns that we picked up in early life can rise to the surface to be acknowledged and released. Hidden beliefs become more conscious and accessible to change. Old conditioning stops running our lives as the transition plays out.

Keep a Rough Transitions Journal

One way to keep track of your journey is to keep a journal. Your journey is important, and this is one way to keep track of your inner and outer experiences. Journaling can help you clarify your thoughts, feelings, and challenges. This is also a good place to record important nocturnal dreams and any insight you may have along the way.

After your transition this will help you keep track of how far you have come. It will also help you make more sense of the journey in hindsight.

5

The Timeless Way

Look up! The skyscrapers are falling. Rapid climate change,
economic collapse, ecological collapse, political instability,
and technological escalation: the only thing we can be sure about
is radical indeterminacy. In the face of this acceleration, we have
choices to make. We can freeze in fear, becoming paralyzed…
Or we can rise onto our surfboards and surf the power of this
wave—particle—wave of change, this tsunami of transformation.
—OCCUPY LOVE

Transition is not random, even though it can be experienced that way, especially with rough and super-rough transitions. In every transition, there is an underlying intention and structure to the journey. This invisible intention and structure comes from a deeper part of our being than the personality, or ego mind, which does not always appreciate a transition.

Even though there is an underlying structure, this does not prevent the experience of transition being highly individual and a unique experience. There are five stages we find on the timeless path: tension, choice-crisis, release, recalibration, and renewal. Naturally, within every journey there has to be a beginning, a middle, and an end. The journey begins with a particular type of tension, then there is a process of transforming that goes on, and then it ends with renewal. The point of the journey is that we change on the inside, and our life on the outside shifts in line with the inner change.

Macro-Level Transition

But before we go any further into the personal transition process, let us take another look from a different angle at the bigger picture of planetary transition. This is important because many individuals are being drawn into transition because of what is happening on Planet Earth right now. The planet is going through a powerful shift; this is not the first time, and it will not be the last.

The last radical planetary transition began around the ending of the last ice age, just under 15,000 years ago. At this time, around one third of the entire planet was under ice. Then, with the thawing of ice, a whole new world opened up for our distant ancestors. Currently, there is a dissolving of an old paradigm to make way for a new world. Because of this there is a great awakening of consciousness happening across the planet. This awakening is vitally important for the future of the planet; it is anchoring a new frequency of light and vibration in the earth. As this happens, there is an acceleration of what we might think of as 'dark' activity on the earth, as well as a clearing of old, dark karma.

The driving force of this global transition is incredible pressure. Galactic and astrological alignments are driving the process, which is currently manifesting also as collective pain and stress. Systemic pain and stress are very necessary at this time, because global change does not happen through people only thinking happy thoughts. Positive affirmations alone will not stop the rainforests from being cut down, nor stop the glaciers from melting.

We are going through a global transition now, and the sheer scale of events seems so big and so overwhelming. (This is why we tend not to think about them too much.) We face vast challenges, including overpopulation, pollution, unpredictable destructive weather patterns, nuclear disasters, the extinction of species and destruction of natural habitats, global warming, the industrialization of our food, genetic modification, fragile global economies, an energy crisis, dwindling essential resources, violence and war, corporate greed, corruption, and a lack of faith in our financial and governing systems.

It is hard to deny that the pressure and demands on the planet are immense and the choices before us are complex. Yet when it boils down to it, we have one choice—to make a meaningful collective shift in consciousness or face extinction.

Although the problems are huge, there are reasons for hope. Cosmic and spiritual forces are at work generating massive impetus for collective change. Pluto, the planet of destruction, transformation, and rebirth is now grinding its way through the earth sign of Capricorn. Pluto entered Capricorn in 2008 and remains there until 2024. Even now, though only part way through, we can see and feel Pluto shaking the foundations of Capricorn and affecting many forms of restrictive structures—in particular, global banking, corporations, and governments. At the same time, we have Uranus, the planet of revolutionary change, in Aries. Uranus entered Aries in 2011 and remains there until 2018. During this time, Uranus moves seven times into an intense square alignment with Pluto, creating tremendous pressure towards systemic change.

This is not the first time this alignment has happened in recent history. A similar astrological alignment happened in the 1960s, which led to a flowering of spiritual awakening. These planets are now in a more tense aspect to each other, setting the scene for considerably greater type of volatile change. Revolutionary Uranus and transformational Pluto have sown the seeds of social rebellion, as witnessed by movements such as Anonymous, Arab Spring, and Occupy. There is a growing awareness in the West among ordinary people that there is something intrinsically wrong with the 'system.' We are more aware of the shenanigans of multinational corporations and the global banking system ever eager for more control and profit.

Governments are little better, and the protectors of democracy are themselves becoming more controlling and secretive. (At the time of writing. I am very mindful of a number of events— drone wars in the borderlands of Afghanistan; Edward Snowden's revelations about the NSA, which opened our eyes to mass spying on ordinary citizens by Western governments; and political-military conflict in Ukraine.) Just as in the film *The Wizard of Oz*, the curtain is being pulled back before our eyes, revealing a controlling elite behind the curtain. They have long been there but only now are becoming more visible. We are living in a time where much that was hidden is being revealed.

The Uranus-Pluto alignments are not the only cosmic energies impacting the planet right now. Pulses of light energy moving from the Galactic Centre are being transmitted down through our sun and onto the earth. These pulses of solar light are having a steady and powerful awakening effect on our higher energy centres. Many high-vibrational souls are now incarnating on the planet, and the sum effect of this is colossal. We are waking up *en masse*.

We are starting to wake up to the fact that war and violence cannot ever promote true peace. We are saying 'no' to activities that destroy the planet and 'yes' to sustainability, inclusivity, and justice. We are becoming more creative and innovative. Multimedia platforms such as TED Talks, a not-for-profit organization promoting a global series of streamed conferences dedicated to 'ideas worth spreading,' are showing the real extent of innovative, solutions-based thinking that is going on in the world. In fact, a multitude of online platforms are giving us a broader picture of world affairs and breaking the stranglehold of the corporate networks that used to shape all our opinions.

There's no lack of ideas and energy to push the boundaries of art, education, farming, science, and practically every other area where solutions are needed. As non-renewable sources of energy decrease, we are moving slowly but surely away from our addictive reliance on fossil fuels. Many organizations are "greening" their operations, and many millions of people are taking a greater responsibility for the environment.

Capitalism, though resilient, is wobbling badly and is in dire need of reinvention. What capitalism has always lacked is a heart. It is heartless because it relies on the misery of debt and requires unrelenting growth. We are more aware of the need for fair trade and responsible consumerism. We are more aware of the need to develop sustainable ways of harvesting or generating energy. Nature, although badly abused, is more resilient than we give it credit for. For instance, after Nagasaki was destroyed by an atomic bomb at the end of World War II, scientists predicted that nothing could grow there for at least 30 years. They were wrong and nature returned much more quickly.

> *We have known for a long time that we must move toward becoming 'one,' toward becoming a global village. We must become an integrated system of life. Knowing that is one thing. Actually doing something about it is another. This crisis is the global opportunity to become what we need to become—and in that, it is the great turning point of humanity.*
>
> — *CAROLYN MYSS*

We are no longer held in the stranglehold of fundamentalist religious belief, as we once were. We are mostly free to explore our own spiritual path, and we have a broad range of choices. Because of this, human consciousness is waking up.

One system that highlights this is Spiral Dynamics, a system mapping the development of human potential and consciousness, from survival and tribal up through empire building, bureaucratic, entrepreneurial, holistic, and beyond to higher levels of complexity and consciousness. These bands are designated by different colours of the rainbow. In recent years, according to this system, two new bands of consciousness have come online. The first band is *yellow*, a level of consciousness that is pragmatic, flexible, embraces solutions, and engages with conversations in order to get things done. The next band is *turquoise*, a level that sees sustainability as the primary issue on the planet. and that this issue is first and foremost a spiritual one.

Turquoise consciousness is more mystical than yellow consciousness, and such individuals believe that in order to change the world they must first change themselves. As more individuals inevitably shift up into the higher octave of yellow and turquoise, we will see global transition turn into global rebirth.

LEVELS OF CONSCIOUSNESS — (SPIRAL DYNAMICS)

TRIBAL PURPLE — Purple is an instinctive way of living that is tribal, shamanistic, and animistic. Here, the universe seems full of helpful and threating powers and spirits. Less than 10 percent of the world operates primarily at purple.

NATIONALISTIC RED — Red views the world as a jungle where only the strong survive. Red values domination, gratification, and rebelliousness. Red is about power, colonialism, territory, acquisition, and empire. Less than 20 percent of the world operates primarily at red.

AUTHORITARIAN BLUE — Blue believes in stability, patriotism, meaning, and purpose. Blue has an absolutist, rigid, and hierarchical way of thinking. Authority, discipline, and rules are essential to well-being and happiness. Also science and the classification and manipulation of the environment are important. Less than 40 percent of the world operates primarily at blue.

ENTREPRENEURIAL ORANGE — Orange is an entrepreneurial, productive, resourceful, and individualistic approach to life. Personal advantage and monetary reward are important. This is about autonomy, status, opportunity, success, and wealth. This is the zone of the free-market economy and corporate strategy. Less than 30 percent of the world operates primarily at orange.

HUMANISTIC GREEN — Green values community, contribution, sharing, consensus, equality, transparency, tolerance, conflict management, love, sharing, a richer inner life, ecology, and coming together for mutual growth. These are the natural hippies that seek communal life. Less than 5 percent of the world operates primarily at green.

SYNERGIZING YELLOW — Yellow is inner directed, pragmatic, and is concerned with synergy, interdependence, viewing the bigger picture, and processing complex ideas. Yellow is able to embrace paradox, see life from different perspectives, and expand choices. Talents are seen as valuable in terms of how they contribute to the whole. This level values flexibility, self-motivation, innovation, and spiritual connectivity. Around 1 percent of the world operates primarily at yellow.

SPIRITUAL TURQUOISE – Turquoise is about the transpersonal, mystical, and is where we find what Maslow called the 'self-actualized.' Turquoise values cooperation, co-creation, and is interested in quantum energy fields, unity consciousness, and working with the unseen. Around 0.1 percent of the world operates primarily at turquoise.

The truth will set you free.
But first, it will piss you off
— *GLORIA STEINEM*

Micro-Level Transition

Personal transitions are timeless; they have been going on ever since humans first lived together on the spiral of life (at purple). Tribal cultures have long understood the importance of certain powerful transition points. Rites of passage have been developed over thousands of years to help humans transition successfully from one stage of life to the next. These mark the passing from one stage to another, or from one social position to another.

Rites of passage have long been effective in helping humans integrate biological and social events such as adolescence, marriage, war, and death. Among the Oglala Lakota, adolescent boys were sent out alone and weaponless into the wilderness to find a guiding vision for their lives. Amongst the Mescalero Apaches, the puberty of young women is a time of celebration for the whole tribe.

Rites of passage are common to every pre-modern culture across the world, yet now, we have lost that understanding. Instead of sending out our young men and women on vision quests to tap into their inner wise adult, we expose them to alcohol, computer video games, violent films, and underage sex. This has no value in helping adolescents transition into adulthood; on the contrary, it helps to keep them stuck in a childish immature ego. It is sad but true that we live in a culture devoid of sacred rites, where we can live to a ripe old age but never truly grow up.

Writer and poet Robert Bly says: 'Boys in our culture have a continuous need for initiation into male spirit, but old men generally do not offer it. The priest sometimes tries, but he is too much a part of the corporate village these days.'

Far too many adults in our modern developed world have remained stuck in childish behaviour. (This is course very different from adults maintaining a childlike quality of innocence, fun, and play.) We have great intellects but no wisdom. The problem nowadays is that there are few elders wise enough to help with the transition into adulthood. What is needed is a map that can be applied to modern day living. This is the way of personal transition.

The timeless path of transition has five stages. These are not necessarily equal in intensity or in length, nor in sharp linear divisions; instead, each phase is like a gently overlapping sphere of experience. It is worth mentioning here that in a transition, our relation to time alters. Time just flies when you are having fun and on your path of adventure, whereas it drags on endlessly when the opposite is true. Also every transition involves a resonance or a pull from the future. The end point of the journey can be felt before it has even begun in earnest.

This is more apparent in a smooth transition where the resonance from the future entices us forward. This resonance also helps guide our choices along the way. We may even have dreams that are a message from the future. In meditation, the Higher Self may whisper of new choices, possibilities, or more specifically of events and people to meet. Synchronicities are set up behind the scenes by our Higher Self, and there is often a greater sense of wonder at the orchestration of unfolding events. A transition shows us experientially the magical nature of the universe, really. We can feel the touch of the sacred in our lives. We form a relationship with soul, light, and a transcendent reality. As we move towards our dreams, we learn to weave our dreams with love, grace, and joy. We manifest our dreams and build, with many others on the earthly plane, a Heaven on Earth.

A rough or super-rough transition is a very different matter. Here, we are like Alice tumbling down the rabbit hole, wondering how deep down it goes. When we are falling, there is a certain inevitability of direction—there is not much we can do here but hold on and hope for the best. The resonance of the end result is still calling us forward (or, as it more often feels, downward), but this usually cannot be consciously felt or known. The pull onwards is unconscious. The reason for this is if the individual knew what was really coming, they would probably run as fast as they could in the opposite direction.

Before a transition happens, the details of the path remain hidden. There might be hints of the path ahead in dreams and through signs in the outer world, but the enormity of what is about to unfold remains a mystery. Even the most intuitive amongst us will not realize what is coming. The Higher Self blocks all information about the pending future, and thus the soul calling has to be more subtle. Events are set up, but there is not the same sense of wonder when they start to manifest. The individual has no idea they are heading into the jaws of a transition, and when it finally erupts there can be a sense of trepidation and alarm.

It is important to realize that when this type of process begins it is hard to turn back— and even if you could, it is never a good idea. Aborting the journey results in a shutting down of possibility, which then results in stuckness. My advice to you here is, even if the path seems dark, do stay with the process. All will pass, and the darkness will turn to light. You are being transformed from a caterpillar to a butterfly. You are not abandoned, even if it feels that way. At the beginning of a transition, it does not matter whether the journey is conscious or unconscious, smooth or rough, the stage has been set and the pieces on the chessboard are about to move.

THE TIMELESS WAY OF PERSONAL TRANSITION

1. **SOUL TENSION** – The transition process starts with a build-up of tension in the body. There are two types of tension: surface tension and soul tension. The former is a pull to fulfil ego needs; the latter is about feeling a soul calling. Soul tension leads to every type of transition, whereas surface tension merely induces more chasing and avoidance. Soul tension is often not recognized for what it is, thus it is usually avoided, ignored, or suppressed.

2. **CHOICE-CRISIS** – If the tension is recognized, embraced, and a life-changing choice is made, then all well and good—a smooth transition ensues. If the tension is recognized, and a bad choice is made, then that is a different matter. If the tension is ignored it builds to a crisis, which allows a trigger or catalyst to enter the drama. This sets the individual off onto a rough or super-rough journey.

3. **RELEASE** – In all forms of transition, people, friends, situations, even possessions can fall away. In a smooth transition this is relatively easy, because the sights are set on a new future. In a rough or super-rough transition, there can be a loss of meaning, purpose, and passion to what went on before. There is also usually a great release of emotions, such as grief at the passing of the old life.

4. **RECALIBRATION** – As the old life drops away in earnest, a new phase emerges where new ground rules apply. If the journey has been consciously chosen, it can seem challenging and exciting. There is the opportunity to shift into something new. If it has not been consciously chosen,

this feels more difficult. A rough or super-rough transition heralds a major reconfiguration of the personality and a dissolving of old ego blocks and defences.

5. **RENEWAL** – In a smooth transition, a new life kicks off in earnest. The dreams and goals are being realized. In a rough transition, this phase heralds an end to challenge, chaos, and crisis. Steadily, there is the gradual dawning of light and a new day. This brings a sense of awakening, purpose, and flow.

Soul Tension

Transition begins with a slow build-up of tension that is nevertheless unrelenting. This tension often goes unrecognized, simply because of the fast-paced nature of our modern world. Most of us would agree that tension of one sort or another is an occupational hazard of life; yet, the kind of tension that creates a life shift is not the same as regular, everyday tension. The latter kind of tension I call 'surface tension,' because it relates to ego-body consciousness needs and desires as well as the pleasure-pain principle. We have needs we want to fulfil, and there are experiences and situations we want to avoid because they feel disconcerting, uncomfortable, or painful. Surface tension is how things get done in the world. We need or want a new washing machine, and we do not have one. This creates tension until the money is found to buy the washing machine, and the tension goes away. This kind of tension can resurface in a thousand and one different ways. Marketers in our consumerist world know about surface tension and use it to sell us stuff.

Soul tension is different. It comes when we are not in touch with our authentic self and not heading in a direction meaningful to our core values. Soul tension is a deep, inner calling to return to our centre, which eventually brings about a new phase of life. The problem is we do not understand soul tension, so we tend to treat it like surface tension. This means we think the tension is about lacking something, so we keep chasing and accumulating even harder.

The point is that soul tension does not go away with the purchase of a new car or when we get that new boyfriend. Instead, we are left confused and even more frustrated when it doesn't resolve the building tension. Soul tension is calling us back to our authentic self. It is a call to release the layers of ego-delusion about ourselves and the world around us. Soul tension is the result of internal conflict and the clamping of life force energy. Putting it as simply as I can: the heart wants one thing and the head another.

Soul tension can be created when we are living the dreams and values of someone else—quite often, this is one of our parents. Soul tension is telling us that we are off-track and unhappy. even though we might tell ourselves quite a different story. Perhaps we work in a job we hate and do it for no other reason than paying the bills. Perhaps we are married to someone who no longer resonates with who we truly are, but we stay together for the sake of an easy life or for the children.

It is not that these reasons for continuing what we are doing are bad or wrong, but at a certain point they will create tremendous internal tension. When we do not feel free to be ourselves this creates inner conflict, which can manifest as stress, a loss of vitality, ill health, frustration, or anxiety. Resisting a soul calling can even manifest as accidents and strange misfortunes—we may not be concentrating properly and start to trip ourselves up. If the pressure to conform is stronger than the desire to be free, then the inner conflict can reach such a point that it feels like the lights are on but nobody is at home. We are no longer really present to our lives.

A rule of thumb is the bigger the transition, the bigger the resistance to the journey. Part of us knows that something big is happening, and another part is terribly afraid of that big change. There are all manner of ways to block or resist a transition, and even though we are resisting we are not always aware of what we are doing. Resistance can be anything from addictive shopping, partying, sex, drinking, to adventure sports. These might work for a short time, but they offer only temporary relief. What we really need to do is turn and squarely meet the soul tension rather than run away from it. Soul tension is asking us to pause, reflect, and rethink our lives. The one thing to note here is that soul tension always seeks release and resolution. Soul tension is a manifestation of the evolutionary impulse, which simply will not go away just because it is inconvenient.

Choice-Crisis

Soul tension builds until we come to a choice point or crisis. If we choose to ignore the tension we experience a building crisis. If we embrace it, then we choose to avert the crisis. We are aware that something needs to change, and we become ever willing to make a life-altering choice. A choice can involve either walking away from a situation or moving directly towards something new. A dream is calling us forward. We feel called to take a new life direction. On this path there will be challenges, but they will all make sense in light of the choice being made. A choice consciously taken most often will lead to a smooth transition. Then again, intense soul tension can drive us impulsively to make a bad choice. This creates a very different set of experiences. When this happens, we find the classic out-of-the-frying-pan-into-the-fire scenario. If we ignore the tension, then we hit a crisis; we do not make a meaningful choice.

There are many reasons for this. Perhaps all of the options seem equally fraught with difficulty and pain, or there are social constraints that seem just too strong to break or leave. Perhaps a calling cuts right across a career path or relationship of many years. We have invested a lot of time and energy into a life, and letting go feels like failure. Perhaps we want to leave but feel afraid because we have no idea what we would do next. When we resist moving forward, we are in some ways like the Biblical Jacob wrestling with the angel. Here, Jacob is wrestling with the life force itself, and unlike the story, we will not be blessed during the struggle. If we avoid taking a much-needed choice, then the window of opportunity will pass and the tension will build without release. This leads to intense internal pressure, discomfort, pain, and outer crisis.

In this place, you may discover no amount of painkillers can numb out a calling back to an authentic life. Tension seeks release, and when it has built up to an explosive level it takes little imagination to guess the end result. In nature, tremendous explosive tension tends to move towards explosive release, through either an earthquake, a tsunami, or a volcanic eruption.

There is an old saying in spiritual circles that if we cannot hear the whispers, then we will hear the shouts. The stage is set for a trigger or catalyst to enter. A catalyst could be considered a soul friend, because he or she or it comes to release us from our present life. According to *Webster's New World College Dictionary*, a catalyst is 'a person or thing acting as the stimulus in bringing about or hastening a result.'

A catalyst can be a person in the form of a lover or protagonist, an accident or illness, or a vision of a different life. A catalyst may not come in the form of one person or one situation; it can also come in a number of converging and conflicting demands. However it comes, the catalyst comes to help us grow up and evolve in some way. Sometimes, the catalyst triggers an existential crisis that leads to a spiritual awakening. The job of the catalyst is purely to move us to the next phase of the journey. One important thing to note here is that for the catalyst to be successful, there must be sufficient impact or force to break through both ego defences and social constraints. Another important aspect to note is that we should avoid getting too attached to a catalyst—when they turn up as a person, they will not tend to hang around once the job is done.

A third thing to note is that a catalyst who is a lover makes poor long-term relationship material. I have sat with several people who have become very attached to the catalyst as a lover. This is a very common pitfall. Even if there has been no physical intimacy, the promise of love itself can be highly addictive. When your life flips or goes into freefall, it is time to let them go. Please remember: the catalyst is just doing a job. They are not there to marry you or love you forever. Nor is it worth blaming them for their actions, or for what they did not do. They are there to serve your soul's journey, not your ego-personality desires and wishes. When the job is done, soul tension begins to turn into objective reality. This leads you to the phase of release.

Release

Whichever way we go, whether it be the smooth, rough, or super-rough route, the stage of release is unavoidable. In a smooth transition, we have chosen the trip and can more easily say goodbye to the old. This does not mean that grief is not there when we let go of people or possessions we love, but it is easier because of the nature of the trip. In a smooth transition we plan the journey, buy the travel guides, and get ready to say goodbye to everyone we love before stepping onto the plane or train. Sometimes we choose the journey, but if the choice is a poor one or an avoidance of the real journey, then we are heading for a rough transition.

In the book *Iron John* by Robert Bly, he describes this phase as 'taking the road of ashes,' which is where people, situations, and possessions suddenly drop away, sometimes without farewell or explanation. When a rough transition becomes a super-rough one, then we feel thrown into an existential crisis. Here, we face the release of our outer life, and at the same time, face an inner loss of hope and meaning. Sometimes, the journey gets so tough that we pass through a dark night of the soul experience, which feels like a deep disconnection from all worldly sources of community, connection, love, or purpose.

This is a fall from grace during which our inner light seems to desert us in our very hour of need, taking with it all sense of guidance and intuition. I say 'seems to desert us,' because this is just the perception and not the reality. This is like Jesus in his moment of agony on the cross saying, 'My God, why have you forsaken me?' We are not abandoned by the life force, although it seems that way. When all the anchors that attach us to our old reality suddenly snap, then we feel lost and adrift. In a rough transition, an emotional abyss opens up. Grief and anger may erupt, along with feelings of confusion, isolation, and depression. We may feel like crying or withdrawing at the drop of a hat, and next minute we may feel aggressive or hopeless.

As our old life falls away, we realize that there is no turning back. The point here is that we should not try and piece our old life back together—it has fallen away for a good reason. This is where we learn the tough lessons of detachment and impermanence. Nothing lasts forever; all things must pass. There is nothing we can do now other than surrender and trust the process. In this way, release takes us happily (or less so) into the next phase of recalibration.

Recalibration

There is an old Chinese proverb, 'Patience is power; with time and patience, the mulberry leaf becomes silk.' Recalibration cannot be rushed. An interesting true story highlights this point. Nikos Kazantzakis, author of *Zorba the Greek*, describes an incident in which he came upon a cocoon cradled in the bark of an olive tree. He arrived just as a butterfly was attempting to emerge. Nikos watched impatiently, and finally he bent over the cocoon and warmed it with his breath, hoping to help the butterfly and speed up the process. The butterfly did indeed emerge more quickly, but in doing so, it also emerged prematurely. Its wings were hopelessly crumpled—they had needed the natural warmth of the sun, not the man's breath. Moments later, the butterfly died in the palm of his hand. 'That little body,' he wrote towards the end of his life, 'is the greatest weight I have on my conscious.'

Recalibration is the all-important re-tuning process. In a smooth transition, recalibration feels like exploring new countryside. We are learning to find our way around and adjust to new game rules. We are looking for new points of reference to find our way around. This is like learning a new language. This usually feels scary and exciting at the same time. Even though we have planned the journey, there is no telling exactly what we will find. Just like visiting a new continent with a guidebook, we find the terrain is not exactly what we expected. Our old map of life no longer works in the same way, and we are attempting to construct a new map of reality.

Our beliefs and values are shifting, and along with it our sense of identity. Recalibration helps separate our values and priorities from those of other people. We can start to dissolve old limiting beliefs. As this happens, we start to see our reality in new ways. Free from the filters of the past, we see new possibilities that were invisible to us previously. New qualities emerge as a result of the journey. Perhaps, our new map of reality now contains more mindfulness, patience, resilience, and adaptability.

In a rough transition, the experience is different. It can feel more like entering a void-like space. We have not come here willingly, and we are still dealing with strong emotions and changing circumstances in our outer world. In a super-rough transition, this phase of recalibration is like pressing the reboot button on a computer: there is nothing much to do but wait.

Another metaphor for this phase is that of the caterpillar entering the darkness of the cocoon. The caterpillar in the cocoon-void senses nothing—no colour, stimulation, or sound. Here, there is a biological release to the attachment of being a caterpillar. Of course, this can be a time of confusion, loneliness, pain, and uncertainty. It can also a time of readjustment and deep transformation. We are releasing an old identity and preparing for renewal. When this happens we begin to discover new attitudes, behaviours, and thoughts that support the emerging new life. We may feel the need to withdraw from friends and family for a time. Taking time out is helpful and often necessary in dealing with emotional and energetic disorientation. This is especially true in a super-rough transition that presents us with an existential crisis. In a rough transition, the crisis is mostly external: we react strongly to external circumstances. In a super-rough transition, the crisis is internal. There is a loss of meaning, belonging, or direction. Here, it is often useful to seek the help of a good therapist, because much internal reshaping work is being done.

We may feel at times that we're walking between two worlds, the material and the spiritual, like the indigenous shamans of old. In the cocoon, we are being prepared to meet parts of ourselves we never knew existed. Here we find what Carl Jung called 'the Shadow,' parts of ourselves that we have repressed or felt were so shameful or terrible that they were flung far away into the unconscious. Of course, we can also throw away positive qualities, such as smartness or creativity, because others did not like them very much. In recalibration, much inner work is being done. Here, in recalibration. we can meet the inner 'wounded child,' as well as the inner 'playful child,' perhaps for the first time. Similarly, a man may encounter his repressed *anima*, his unconscious feminine, and a woman may encounter her repressed *animus*, her unconscious masculine. This sounds dramatic, but it is also usually deeply healing.

In a super-rough transition, we meet the dark night of the soul experience. (The experience could be more aptly called a dark night of the ego, which can last for days, weeks, or months, or in some cases years.) The dark night comes to crack open the hard shell of the ego in order to allow in more light. It should be noted that in a super-rough transition, the intuition is often disconnected for a time. This is because there is so much intense work happening that our energy fields become a little muddy and disturbed. This prevents our intuition or gut feeling from operating properly until the inner work is completed.

During recalibration, the ego becomes steadily reconfigured into a more fluid and positive sense of self. We do not need to know how this happens, just to experience it happening. This is part of the great mystery of the transition process. In recalibration, you might feel the need to just be with yourself or, conversely, you might want to be more in the company of certain kinds of people. If you seek aloneness, the lesson here is to enjoy aloneness. Recalibration prepares us for the more outgoing phase of renewal.

Renewal

In a smooth transition, we have followed a dream or vision and bravely followed our heart into the unknown. Our courage has led us to step towards a desire or dream. Whether the dream turns out the way we expected is not the point; as a result of the journey, we will feel more capable, confident, and resourceful than before. We have metaphorically sailed our boat out of the safe harbour and navigated the open sea. We now know that the harbour no longer defines us, and the world seems bigger than before. In a smooth transition, there may seem to be little distinction between recalibration and renewal—we are so focused on the outer journey, we may not fully appreciate all the internal shifts that have taken place. In a rough or super-rough transition, renewal feels like the emergence of spring after deep and bitter winter. Renewal is possible because of the transformational work done in recalibration. Renewal is not instantaneous; more often it is a gradual event, like the dawning of a new day. At the beginning of renewal, we are still adjusting to the loss of the old and to the revelations of the new. The pain of the past has vaporized in the morning light of renewal, and the heart has the space to breathe again. We have a greater sense of freedom and possibility, and any confusion or sense of stuckness is replaced by a clarity and flow. Now, we can start to meditate on what is truly worthy and important in life. In a super-rough transition, the intuition and gut instinct have been disconnected and now resurface with greater depth and clarity. Where there was a dark night, now there is light. Many previously held ideas about life or spirituality have dropped away to reveal a deeper level of being or truth.

As we go deeper into renewal, there is greater stability and the emergence of a new psychological space. There is a deeper connection to the spirit within and a growing sense of revelation. We have an increased need for integrity and truthful self-expression. During the transition, there was little sense of synchronicity and flow. These return, and over time we increasingly find ourselves in the right place at the right time. We start to meet the right people and the perfect opportunities. We have a deepening sense of trust in self and life. The world may continue to feel dream-like for a time, as we shift our core vibration to higher states of love and joy. Our consciousness is still being transformed, even in renewal. Speaking in terms of Spiral Dynamics, we may have experienced a shift within a band, or made a radical step into the lower rungs of the next band up. Shifting into a new band is a massive leap in consciousness and hails an exciting evolutionary period. Anything can happen now, and grace and miracles seem more commonplace. Our authentic self has moved us to explore the world in a new way. What happens next is anyone's guess!

PART TWO

The Timeless Way of Transition

6

The Ground Trembles

There is a candle in your heart, ready to be kindled.
There is a void in your soul, ready to be filled.
You feel it, don't you?

— *RUMI*

Author and psychiatrist M. Scott Peck once wrote that life is difficult, and only when we embrace that fact can we ever seek to transcend it. Some people seek perfection in their lives, but perfection is a completed state, the very antithesis of growth, opening, learning, and awakening. Life is difficult and comes with challenge and tension. To avoid challenge does not mean we avoid tension. If we retreat from life and avoid desire or passion, this does not stop us from feeling tension. We feel tension when we are in a job that is dull or stressful, a relationship that is stuck or too demanding, or at a more material level, if we are not driving the right brand of car or living in the right location.

In everyday life, tension is generated when a need or want hits up against an external block or internal resistance. We want something and do not have it, or we do not want something and cannot get rid of it. This is what I call 'surface tension.' It is linked to the pleasure-pain principle: pleasure entices, and pain repels. Surface tension is how things move and get done in the world—basically, no tension equals no motivation, no momentum, no action. Without a degree of tension, there would be little incentive to shop, eat, wash the dishes, build, or make love. Of course, too much surface tension and we feel stressed, overwhelmed, and unable to meet all of life's demands. Not enough surface tension, and we feel so chilled or relaxed that nothing happens at all.

Some surface tension is to be expected when living in the everyday world. This level of tension, when it is high, creates lots of change but never leads to a transition. The ego knows about change but does not know about transformation. A transition is initiated by a deeper level of force, which can generate what I call 'soul tension.'

100

Soul tension is very different from our ego's chasing, accumulating, and avoidance strategies. Lines of soul tension force can be seen in the hard aspects in the natal birth chart. Soul tension also starts to activate with the transits of certain celestial bodies. Chiron, Pluto, Saturn, and Uranus transits are all important ones. To understand current or pending soul tension in your chart, you need to consult an experienced astrologer.

Soul tension manifests when a calling to return to living an authentic life collides with ego defences and cultural-family rules or other social conventions. (I could spend a whole chapter trying to define an authentic life. The point is that if you do not know what it is, you are probably not living it.) Soul tension is a whole different dimension and much harder to deal with, since now it's not about the car we want to drive, the promotion we deserve, or the person we want to date.

Soul tension is a feeling that something is wrong, missing, or out of kilter. What that something is can be hard to explain or describe. Perhaps the tension points to something we have yet to experience in the future. Because it is hard to put our finger on the issue, and since we do not like to feel confused or uncomfortable, we often seek to avoid the feeling through busyness, distraction, or addiction. If this is the case, we can be sure of one thing: we are living superficially and off track in our lives. We may be married to the wrong person, working in the wrong career, living in the wrong country, or hanging out with the wrong people.

When we resist the calling, soul tension will build. If we mistake soul tension for surface tension, we will continue to feel frustrated and unhappy. Soul tension is slow-building but often incredibly strong. The important aspects of soul tension to note are:

- The physical world is made up of vibrating energy;
- The same is true of our internal psychic world;
- A soul calling is a deep current of vibrating energy;
- Resistance to this deep current creates soul tension;
- Tension is resolved through crisis or by aligning with the soul calling.

Soul tension is calling us to a different life; yet, the problem is that, even if we are fortunate enough to recognize the issue, we may still not do anything about it. There are many reasons for this. Perhaps we are waiting for the right moment, and it never comes. Perhaps we lack the courage to act or feel unable to do so in some way. Perhaps the calling feels too big or grand, or we feel confused about our next step, or we feel there are just too many demands in the way. Soul tension is basically telling us that there is a disconnection from self—we no longer know ourselves and, instead, cling to masks, labels, and roles. Soul tension is a symptom of resisting the soul, which asks nothing less of us than we dive into the journey where we will discover our as yet unknown inner potential and light.

> *If you want to find the secrets of the universe,*
> *Think in terms of energy, frequency, and vibration.*
>
> — *NIKOLA TESLA*

What Is Soul Calling?

A soul calling involves trust and surrender. We have to trust a deeper part of ourselves that knows where we are going. A soul calling is not satisfied with us just sticking a toe into the water; we either sign up for the entire journey and see it through, or we are a spectator standing on the sidelines thinking about the journey. A soul calling is calling us to a higher state of presence, vibration, and flow. The problem is that we live in a low-vibrating world that is largely spiritually unaware. A soul calling is an energetic impulse to change the way we process the world. It is also a pull to a new sense of belonging and direction. How this energetic impulse is received and understood depends on how open or resistant we are. As already mentioned, resistance is how we block or divert a soul calling.

In his brilliantly insightful book, *The Path of Least Resistance,* author Robert Fritz describes how, for generations, cows have walked around the hills of Boston, Massachusetts, gradually forming cow paths. A cow would simply wander through the landscape, avoiding rocks and sharp inclines, and taking the route that seemed easiest in the moment. Over time, these cow paths became more clearly defined. When the planners came to build the roads in the 17th century, they just followed the simple logic of the cow and used the existing cow paths to plan their roads. This was because they knew the cows were simply following the route of least resistance.

Just as a cow will follow the path of least resistance, so too water flowing through the earth or electricity flowing through circuitry will take the path of least resistance. Everything is energy, and energy seeks to follow the path of least resistance. Money is energy—it flows from hand to hand, through high street shops and supermarkets, and more invisibly through online businesses, banking systems, and offshore tax havens. Resistance to money flow comes from activities such as restrictive government regulations and taxation, which encourage money to be secreted away in tax-free havens.

All forms of energy follow the path of least resistance. This is why people, who are living energy systems themselves, walk through doors rather than climb through windows to enter a building. It is also why traffic flows away and around congestion rather than seeks to move through it. Just as traffic seeks to find the easiest route, so do other energy flows. If a pedestrian route is blocked, then typically an alternative route is sought. If a block seems temporary, then we can always wait for it to clear. Again the choice is about how to move towards our destination with the minimum of energy expenditure. Where a block is permanent, then energy will flow around the impediment to find another way. Water will flow around logs damming a river, electricity cables will be re-routed, and a hacker will find ways around blocking security measures. A soul calling will follow the path of least resistance.

What we are reluctant to touch often seems the very fabric of our salvation.

— *DON DELILLO*

The Nature and Structure of Resistance

In life, we need a certain amount of structure. Sometimes, structures are valuable for a time and then as life progresses prove less so. A structure may support our ego's wants and needs but not the deep yearning of the soul. Where this happens, the structure has become spiritually 'negative' because it resists the light of a soul calling.

In the outer world, there are three main structures that hold together our reality: culture; large systems, such as government, law, and corporations; and last but not least, family. These structures are themselves influenced by the all-important factors of time and place.

For instance, America in the 1940s had different rules around what was allowed or not allowed. The 1940s were the war and post-war era, when the nuclear bomb had been invented and used. The television was now available to the public. The average salary was $1,300 per year. This was the heyday of actors such as Fred Astaire, Rita Hayworth, Humphrey Bogart, and Elizabeth Taylor. On the radio, this was the time of Ella Fitzgerald and Glen Miller. Hollywood began to drive the fashion industry. The book *1984* by George Orwell was published. In this decade, flower power was unthinkable, the information-virtual revolution had not begun, and the civil rights movement was still some decades away.

Fast forward to America in the 1980s, and we have video games, aerobics, camcorders, the rise of the billionaire, double-digit inflation, the average salary was $16,000 a year, there were AIDS and the 'war on drugs,' and ET phoned home. Now, at the beginning of the 21st century, American culture has globalization, Monsanto, 9/11, the election of a black president, the internet, iPads, 3-D films, NSA spying scandals, and the emergence of China as a new economic power.

Shifts in the level of culture affect all the levels below. Culture is the bigger picture that a soul calling has to contend with. The more open and liberal the culture, the easier it is for a soul calling to do its work. Cultures that are closed and authoritarian make it harder for the light of the soul to gain expression in the world.

Next, we have large structures such as governments, corporations, and educational systems. Every system has rules, spoken and unspoken. In your average office, there will be rules about everything, from time keeping to dress code to what is appropriate to display on your desk and how you can use the internet. On a construction site there are different rules, which are more about health, safety, and security of materials and premises.

Spiritual organizations have rules. I knew a man who was a devotee of an Eastern religion. He had been raised in the religion, since his parents were both converts from an early age. Although he had many friends and found the community supportive, it was not so helpful when he was going through a possible nervous breakdown. He went to his guru, whose advice was to simply 'chant harder,' which, although it was completely in line with the thinking within the organization, made him feel worse. He had to go outside the system to find any real help and support.

This brings us to sub-groups, such as friends or other support groups. Some groups are open, inclusive, and supportive, while others may be less so. Peer pressure can be subtle and not so subtle. Some groups may be very supportive until a new major factor such as a soul calling comes into the mix. Some groups break apart as a result of one individual following a soul calling.

This brings us to the next layer, which is the most intimate, durable, and often the most resistant to a soul calling: family. Families have rules. A family living in tribal Afghanistan will have different ways of interacting and have completely different taboos compared with a middle class family living in London. Even within the same culture, there can be great variations in thinking and behaviour within families living in the same part of town—or the same street, for that matter. One family may feel fundamentally optimistic, whereas another family living a few streets away may be depressed and gloomy.

In the outer world, there is a great tapestry of interweaving structures that a soul calling has to navigate. Some of these are extremely resistant to a soul calling and might as well made out of green kryptonite (which we know is deadly to Superman). If we are unfortunate to find ourselves held within such a system, we feel robbed of our powers of clear thinking, imagination, and intuition, and instead play small or rebellious. This can equally apply to family systems and peer groups. Outer structures can resist a soul calling, but often this reflects inner egoic structures that can be equally as blocking or rigid.

> *If you bring forth that which is within yourselves,*
> *That which you possess will save you.*
> *If you do not find that within yourselves,*
> *That which you do not possess will kill you.*
>
> — *GOSPEL OF THOMAS*

Just as we need external structure to give our reality stability, we also need internal structure, which we call our 'core beliefs and values.' These are held within a larger psychic structure we call the 'ego,' or 'personality.' (We explored the stages of ego development in Chapter Two). Inner structures are not made of bricks and mortar, but they can be just as enduring. We need ego structures to cope with and move through the world.

For individuals on a path of self-inquiry, growth, and awakening, a flexible ego is most useful. This is because the demands of the external world change and we need an ego that can adapt to new situations and conditions. Also, the demands of our inner light, or soul, change because there are times when it seems dormant or less interested in what we are doing, and there are other times when it more urgently seeks to move us in some way. In this way, the light of the soul can feel like the waxing and waning of the moon. It moves in cycles and is not consistent. This is not because the soul is in any way linked to the moon; the point is that the soul has its own rhythms.

Our knowledge of soul has mostly been lost, due to our obsession with rational, analytical thinking. The less we are exposed to spiritual practice or personal development work, the more inflexible and distrusting will be our ego, because we are not educated to understand the mysteries of soul. Since our outer structures of culture, large systems, and family are not in synch with soul, we tend to grow egos or personalities that are completely out of synch with our heart and soul.

The more inflexible our ego, the more 'negative' and resistant we will seem. Parts of us can remain stuck and immature for many years. As a child, having a tantrum was part of growing up; as an adult, having tantrums can be problematic. For a child being too smart or too adventurous or too anything can be a problem. One way the growing ego deals with this is to jettison any undesirable qualities. This becomes part of what has been called 'the shadow.' The more we jettison our gifts and abilities, the more 'negative' our personality, or ego, will tend to be.

An inflexible and negative ego is a challenge for a soul calling. For instance, a new dream or highly desirable goal can collide with an old belief about how life works and what is possible for us to achieve in the world. It can also find itself blocked by a feeling of duty to an existing job or relationship. The calling to leave an existing way of life can easily be countered by a fear of change and a strong desire to remain comfortable and secure. Resistance is like the brake pedal of a car, whereas a calling is the accelerator pedal. Of course, we need both. The brake pedal slows us down and allows us to take life at a reasonable pace, but too much resistance is like driving a car with the brake on all the time. If the power of the brakes is stronger than the desire to move forward, then we grind to a halt. The price we pay for living this way is two-fold: firstly, nothing much happens and our lives lack aliveness and all hope of revitalization; secondly, we are in danger of aborting the whole process if it goes on for too long. This is not a healthy state of affairs. It means staying stuck at some level emotionally, mentally, and spiritually. When this happens, deep down we know we have turned down an important opportunity as the window of opportunity passes.

TYPICAL RESISTANCE PATTERNS

BLAME – We are taught to blame as a means of self-protection and self-preservation. It seems to be the case that blaming others allows us to avoid taking responsibility for our life. When we are blaming, it is impossible to appreciate at the same time.

BUSYNESS – We can seek to block or divert tension by focusing on constant doing and busyness. Busyness leads to burnout, which is never a great way to go in life.

COMPARISON – We are taught from a young age to compare and contrast. It is never wise to compare our looks, talents, or journey with those of another person. When we compare, it is impossible to accept where we are in life.

CONFLICT – We are taught to defend ourselves by being right. Arguing leads to conflict, which is a powerful way to divert our energy and prevent radical change. When we are in conflict, we are in fight-or-flight mode and it is hard to pause for breath before speaking or acting.

CONTROL – We are taught to try and control our lives. If we try to do that, though, we will simply become dull and unbearable and others will avoid us. Control is the antithesis of trust.

DOUBT – We are taught to doubt, and excessive doubt will close the heart and stunt the mind. Doubt is a many-headed hydra that closes us to real feedback or engagement.

DRAMA – We are surrounded by drama—in the newspapers, on the TV, and at the cinema and theatre. We can create drama in our lives to avoid following our soul's calling. Drama can be an addictive resistance pattern, which does not really allow for more slow-moving mindfulness and reflection.

FANTASY – We live in a world of virtual reality and easy escape into fantasy. Fantasy is a resistance to life and is different from dreaming or vision. Fantasy clouds the mind and stops us from getting clear about our intentions or next steps.

FEAR – This is perhaps the mother of all resistance patterns. There are many variations on this theme: fear of the unknown, fear of failure, fear of condemnation, fear of success, fear of intimacy, fear of your own light and power. There is an old saying, 'Where there is fear there is power.' When we embrace fear, it can become fuel for the journey.

GREED – We are encouraged to mindlessly consume and accumulate. This helps us to live heavily on the earth and avoid what is really meaningful. Often, beneath greed is unhappiness. We cannot be greedy and generous at the same time.

GUILT – We are taught guilt from a young age. Religion teaches guilt. Families teach guilt. Guilt believes in punishment and suffering. When we feel guilty, it is hard to give any importance to our own values, dreams, and visions.

HELPLESSNESS – We can be taught perceived helplessness from a young age. This is kept going with thoughts such as, I cannot do this, I cannot cope, or life's too hard. Helplessness does not allow us to set achievable goals nor develop any form of self-reliance.

OVERATTACHMENT – We know there is healthy bonding and there is unhealthy attachment. Overattachment creates a fusion or clinging to people, circumstances, possessions, status, or an outmoded sense of identity. Fusion makes it hard to let go and develop a healthy sense of love and personal responsibility.

OVER-RATIONALIZATION – We are taught to think, and a tricky form of resistance comes from overthinking and being stuck in the head. Staying in the moment and feeling the response of the heart is hard with over-rationalization.

PERFECTIONISM – We are encouraged to be perfect. Perfection is the opposite of spontaneity, growth, and adventure. Knowing that everything is imperfectly perfect is almost impossible for perfectionists.

PLEASING – We can resist following our heart because of a desire to make everyone around us happy first. This is completely impossible and keeps us stuck in unhappy patterns and situations. Focusing on pleasing others makes it hard for us to say no and set healthy boundaries.

RESCUING – We can resist our own path by overly focusing on rescuing others or solving other people's problems. There are times when it feels right to help; there are other times when we must simply allow other people to have their experiences and trust they will find the right way in the situation.

SECURITY – One of the biggest resistances we face comes from a deep need for security. When we are living a comfortable life, it takes a lot of soul tension to push us out of the nest.

SELF-ATTACK – We are taught to attack and criticize ourselves when we are faced with perceived danger. 'Better the devil you know' is the motto here. Self-criticism and self-attack programs gives us no peace of mind and keeps us playing very small in life.

SHAME – This tells us we are flawed, defective, or not good enough in some way. Shame is connected to guilt and embarrassment. Shame is endemic in Western society and disconnects us from our authentic self, which knows no shame.

*It takes a lot of courage to release the familiar and seemingly secure,
to embrace the new. But there is no real security in what is no longer
meaningful.
There is more security in the adventurous and exciting, for in movement there is life, and in change there is power.*

— *ALAN COHEN*

In my own case, in the summer of 2010, before my transition began, I felt an-
chored in a stable relationship, a gorgeous home, and work I loved. Yet despite
this, somewhere deep down, I knew there was a lack of challenge and adventure
in my life. Instead, my life felt loving yet unfulfilled. It was like there was an itch
I did not know how to scratch. As the soul tension increased over time, I tried
many ways to deal with it—coaching, playing more sport, delegating some of
my work, taking on new projects, and going on more holidays. But nothing really seemed to make any difference, and the tension kept building.

Even though I had been through a rough transition before, I did not recognize
the signs. This was a super-rough transition, and I had no reference points for this
particular journey. If I had known what was coming, I know I would have done
everything I could to have avoided that journey.

I still loved my partner, Ursula. Yes, we had challenges, but on balance I believed we would always stay together. In my work, I had dedicated many years to
building and growing Alternatives as a successful not-for-profit business promoting self-help and spiritual authors in the heart of London. I had made many
friends there and considered it to be more like a family than people I worked
with. I had dedicated the best working years of my life to Alternatives, and could
see no real reason to leave. Also, I had no idea what else I would do in the world.
For these reasons and more, I resisted the transition.

Then, in early 2009, inner tension began to manifest in the outer structures of
my life. It started with a game of squash that left me with a painful back issue that
lasted the whole year. I saw masseurs and osteopaths, but nothing seemed to help.
Then, several months later, I developed a tooth infection that gave me agony for
some weeks. During this time, my stepson, Ian, started to go through his teenage
time of transition, and this all added to the difficulty of the mix. There were also
some odd financial challenges that put me under pressure to work harder and
earn more money. However, it was not all tough going. My first granddaughter,
Eva, was born in August 2009, and her birth felt like the arrival of a happy light
in the family system.

To top it all off, sometime that same year, I had a personal coaching session where my coach (the same person who was my squash partner earlier in the year) rather forcibly pushed me to talk about my goals until I eventually replied, 'To get to these goals, I would have to leave my partner and Alternatives, and that is something I am not prepared to do!' I have no recollection of this conversation, but my coach still puts hand on heart swearing that this is what I said. I guess I went completely unconscious afterwards and just carried on with the nuts and bolts of my life—that is until a radical transition hit the following year, and this statement turned out to be a self-fulfilling prophecy.

When you have exhausted all possibilities, remember this: you haven't.
— *THOMAS EDISON*

Handling Soul Tension

The problem with soul tension is that we are not taught about it, and most of us cannot recognize it when it comes. Hopefully, this is something that this book will remedy. Time and space away from a busy life for reflection is often important. Sometimes, this is not enough, and you need to get some help. Finding a good counsellor or coach, someone who is experienced in the dimension of soul, can be invaluable. During my own transition, I realized that I needed more clarity, insight, and support, so I signed up for weekly transpersonal counselling. Although it was too late to avoid a super-rough transition, it has still proved immensely helpful and supportive during a period of rapid change.

One of the advantages of gaining outside help is that you open yourself up to new forms of feedback. Feedback helps us make accurate adjustments, such as rebalancing our car wheels or adjusting spinal vertebrae. Feedback is how systems naturally adjust. Feedback is what keeps a plane from London to New York on course. Great feedback takes account of our whole situation—our challenges, values, and goals. Great feedback is non-judgemental, constructive, objective, timely, and truthful. We trust it because the person giving the feedback has no emotional attachment to how you are living your life; they just want the best for you. (Please note: I am not referring here to feedback in the form of a work appraisal. This is because the person giving the feedback is usually putting the interests of the system over and above your own.)

On a positive note: a transition is a powerful time, and this is when soul friends turn up. These are people we share a soul affinity with, or who have been contacted by our Higher Self to enter our lives for a specific time or purpose.

They may remain connected to us in one form or another for years after the transition. This is another aspect of the great mystery of transition. These soul friends can show up and offer unexpected help, support, or messages from the soul.

In every important transition, human angels have showed up in the form of a wonderful friend, or an amazing teacher or mentor, a new lover, or in the form of professional help. It is important to be aware of soul friends and be on the lookout for them. (We also meet soul friends in the next stage as catalysts, but that is a different type of soul friend.) Perhaps the best piece of advice I can give at this stage is to simply hang out with the tension. What I mean by this is: Do not avoid it, deny it, or run from it. Why? Because this is the fuel of the whole process.

When you hang out with tension, you can learn to distinguish surface tension from soul tension. Perhaps you change your job or relationship, and the tension goes away. Then you know it is surface tension. But if it comes back quickly, then you know it is soul tension. Recognition is just one part of the equation; what to do about it is next. Firstly, it is probably easiest to look at some of the external factors that might be blocking a soul calling. This next bit takes courage, because external structures do not give way through just thinking loving thoughts (although this can, of course, help)! Perhaps, it is time to stand up to a bullying boss, let go of a dull job, say no to a partner's constant demands, stop fitting in with the demands of your family, let go of a critical friend, or take steps to downsize and simplify your life.

As you can see, courage is the pivotal force to move forward. Every transition demands courage, yet the risks are great—friends may not agree with you anymore, your family may not like it, and you may feel lost and confused for a time. This is all part of growing up and taking back your power and learning to shape your reality.

On the other hand, perhaps it is time to consider your dreams and what you truly want to do with your 'one precious life.' It might be time to look at what inspires, moves, or touches you. Soul tension can build when the leap to a new life seems incredibly daunting. I know this one, as I have stood in this place two or three times in my life. The issue is that we want to leave something, a relationship or a job, but we are afraid of the void and we do not know how to move forward. Also, we might have invested time, money, and energy and do not want to let go of all of that.

Again, support and time for reflection can be invaluable. Timing is also important. Perhaps, we are still building skills, or internal strength, or the willingness to just do it. There can be a lack of supporting external structures in place.

This is like standing at the edge of a chasm and looking across to the other side where you want to go—the gap seems too wide. Sometimes, we learn to swim by jumping into the deep end. Sometimes, we need to take some swimming lessons first! If the dream is strong enough, then a way will be found and the resources to make the journey will present themselves. This is all part of the great mystery of transition. If the journey is not made, then a rough or super-rough transition will come along and give you a much-needed nudge or shove.

CHANGING A NEGATIVE LIFE SCRIPT

- Write down the story of your life as if it were a book, play, or film. What is the title of this story? What is the main theme of your story? Is it around stuckness, self-sabotage, suffering, or pain? Or perhaps it is about forgiveness, redemption, and hope? Could it be about the forces of light versus dark, or from disempowerment to hero's journey?

- Write about the central character in your story. What is the background, the culture, and family like? What are the different roles and functions of the supporting cast? What are the recurring patterns, obstacles, and triumphs? Why would someone choose to play this role? Whatever the challenges, they point to a chosen life theme. Did any of the life themes in Chapter One make you tingle or excited or afraid? What would you love your story to be about—perhaps artist, healer, hero, divine masculine or feminine, lover, magician, teacher or sage?

- If you could rewrite the script of this book, play, or film, what new theme would you choose? If you have a painful script involving anxiety, depression, suffering, or misery, what would you choose instead? Realize that you are not the victim of this script; you always have choices, and you do not have to choose the painful route. How could the story be more loving and enjoyable?

- Make a list of the things you would like to see changed in your life. From this list, select a couple of things on which to focus initially. Ask yourself:

Is this an important issue in my life? If so, what changes can I begin to make?

- If the changes you want to make seem too big, then rewrite your script in stages. Small steps are often more manageable than big leaps of faith. This allows your unconscious mind to adjust to the transition you are seeking to make without running into too much resistance. So if you want to change your script to having more joy, then imagine first what is possible before changing it to what seems improbable at this stage. For instance, changing your script by dropping certain duties that you no longer enjoy could be possible. Then you have the space to do something you have never tried before. If something seems impossible, ask yourself the question, Why is this impossible for me, when it is possible for other people? When you have achieved the possible, you can move towards the improbable. In the equation, always take into account what it costs you not to make the change and also to make the change.

- Are you willing to pay the price of changing your script? It might mean some of the people in your life will no longer want to be in your story. It will probably also mean that new people who want to take part will enter your story further down the line. Changing a life script can begin a transition process. Are you willing to take the journey, even though at this stage you have no idea where it will lead?

The Other-Worldly Language of Transition

Transitions are complex processes, and we cannot always work out what soul tension is trying to tell us with only our conscious mind. This is why it is important to also take note of the messages and communications from our unconscious mind. Our unconscious mind is closer to the soul than the conscious mind. The soul can speak through our unconscious mind. It does this through physical sensations, intuitions, and through our nocturnal dreams. When we are asleep, our conscious mind cannot interfere and we are more open to a direct communication with deeper parts of the psyche.

'Dreaming is non-essential when it comes to survival as a body but is essential with regard to our development and evolution as metaphysical beings,' according to Jeffrey Sumber, who studied global dream mythology at Harvard University and Jungian dream interpretation at the Jung Institute in Zurich.

One way to work with dreams is to start a dream journal. This can be a fantastic memory aid and source of insight, although, at first, keeping one does involve a certain amount of self-discipline. There are some good reasons why this is helpful. Dreams let us play out painful or puzzling experiences in our outer life in a safe way. Dreams often speak to us about our emotions, since studies have shown that the part of the brain that control emotions is also the same part of the brain that controls our dreams. So dreams also convey a depth of information about the emotional life of the unconscious that the conscious mind has little awareness of.

Repressed emotions are often a major factor in the build-up stage of transition, so bringing painful emotions to awareness can help us adjust our lives before we hit an unnecessary crisis. Once the habit of listening to our dreams is instilled, it gets easier and the information becomes increasingly deeper. This is because our soul gets the message that we are consciously paying attention at last! Then the dreams get really interesting. The unconscious speaks in symbols, metaphors, and story, and it can present literal information. Dreams can be prophetic, giving us essential information about our current path. In smooth transitions, they can tap into different timelines and show us glimpses of our highest possible future. Sometimes, dreams come as warnings to alter something or change course. One dream I had came as a warning not to take a trip to Mexico, that if I did I would be attacked in some way. I was about to visit America and was considering hiring a car to drive across the border. Needless to say, I cancelled this plan. Dreams can reveal unresolved fears that are hidden to a large extent from the conscious mind. They can also reveal solutions to problems we are facing in our outer life. Dreams are an opportunity for loved ones who either live far away or are deceased to come and visit us. Our authentic self can also speak to us through our dreams. Because a dream is something we remember when we first wake up, it is important to journal our dreams so that we can capture and reflect on any important information before it fades back into the recesses of the unconscious mind.

WRITE DOWN YOUR NIGHT DREAMS

- Keep your transition journal next to your bed, along with a pen. Alternatively, keep an audio recording device by your bed so that when you wake up you can record what you remember. If you dream and wake up in the night, record your dream immediately.

- Date your entry, and write down everything down that you can recall. Try to include every detail; scenarios, places, sensory information such as sounds and colours, characters, faces, any discussions you have, times, and seasons of the year are all potentially meaningful. If you have dreams with recurring themes, note that down also.

- Think of every character, situation, or important object in the dream being a reflection of a part of your psyche. Notice which aspects you feel comfortable with and which ones you feel ill at ease with.

- Note all the emotions you felt during the dream, such as anxiety when being chased or exhilaration when flying, or happiness when meeting up with friends or loved ones. What is the emotional undertone of the dream? Explore recurring thoughts or themes in dreams. Recurring thoughts, such as *They are going to harm me, I am not safe, I am lost, or I do not understand,* may reflect how you are feeling about your outer life.

- Explore the metaphorical messages of the dream. If you are unsure, go into meditation and recall the dream. Now ask different characters in the dream questions to find out what they are doing and why, and also any messages they have for you. Explore any powerful symbols in the same way. Try dialoguing with them, or even see if they are willing to shape-shift into something more revealing. Do not rely on universal interpretations of symbols. The meaning of each symbol is unique to the context of the dream.

- Explore the literal messages of the dream. Does the dream reflect anything going on in your life at the moment? Are there any prophetic messages about your future in the dream? Remember: you are the best interpreter of your own dreams. There are no set rules. No information is insignificant, although some aspects may feel more important than others.

7

A Knock at the Door

There is some kiss we want with our whole lives,
the touch of spirit on the body.
Seawater begs the pearl to break its shell.

— RUMI

In a transition, soul tension builds at a slow yet unrelenting pace, like a pressure cooker left on a stove with constant heat. Without due care and attention, the food can overcook and even burn. The issue here is that pressure cookers are built to withstand high pressure for long periods of time, but human beings are not. Individuals have limits—emotionally, mentally, physically, and even spiritually.

Just as we have inner limits, so too do the outer structures; just as internal ego structures feel the pressure of soul tension, so too do outer structures of friends, family, and work. If the calling is strong, it will push through all inner and outer resistance. Ego structures can wobble, crack, or break apart, as can marriages, friendships, and even families. In this stage, soul tension continues to build gradually and relentlessly until something shifts or give way.

The Threshold of Choice

Soul tension brings us to a place of choice which, when all the story and details are taken away, boils down to either continuing on our existing trajectory or choosing something different. The choice for something new could mean first walking away from something such as a career or marriage, which then opens the way for something new to happen. On the other hand, we can choose to step more directly into, say, a new business or travel plan. The choice to stay on the existing path is also a choice to say no to anything new. There are many reasons for such a choice, including, as the old saying goes, 'Better the devil you know.' Perhaps we have no idea what else to do; there are too many choices, too many risks. Or it could be a question of timing or lack of resources or confidence.

Then again, it could be just a matter of being too comfortable. When this happens, change can only enter the equation when we get a little uncomfortable. Gregg worked as a journalist in his twenties. After working in this field for the better part of a decade, he reached a threshold where he began to feel a 'calling' to quit his job and become a freelance writer. He did not follow this calling for some years. Gregg says of the moment he made the choice to follow his heart: 'Eventually, the prospect of emotional and even financial turmoil, the disapproval of others, and the various conniptions of change seemed preferable to the psychological death I was experiencing by staying put ... at which point I followed a bit of cowboy wisdom: "When your horse dies, get off!"'

Gregg's story beautifully illustrates the dilemma facing many people at this point in a transition. We wait until the build-up of soul tension overwhelms our resistance, and we just take the next step, In Gregg's case, it worked out very well, as he went on to being a successful author on a great book called *Callings*. This has helped open up a whole new level of work, and he is now in demand as a lecturer and public speaker on the subject.

Sometimes, we need a little help from the Universe to take the next step. Our soul can whisper to us not only through our nocturnal dreams but through other people, situations, and nature. Gabriela had been contemplating a major choice for some time, and she told me about an incident after dropping her children off at school. 'It was an autumn day. I remember lots of trees, and I walked up to one horse chestnut tree. I remember it, because it was the only tree that for some reason still had its leaves; all the others were bare. I stood in front of this tree and was totally captivated by its energy. As I stood there, it was almost like the tree was speaking to me, and I heard a voice in my head that told me my life would never be the same again. Then the wind picked up, and it started to blow most of the leaves off the tree. I just stood there, witnessing this. Time seemed to stand still, and as I stood there tears started to stream down my face. The tree seemed to be a powerful metaphor for my life, and watching the leaves being blown down the street by the wind told me it was time to let go of my old life. I separated from my husband two weeks later, and this put me on a completely new course in my life.'

Sometimes, the choice is not so much about leaving something but more directly exploring something new. I knew Sandra for several months as housemates before she started to talk about going on a big life adventure. She wanted to go to India, and she had been thinking about it for some time before she finally decided to go.

I asked her about this choice point. She said: 'I went to India because I was on a spiritual journey, and I was keen to shake things up entirely in my life. My decision to go to India was a radical thing to do, and some people could not really understand my real need to do it. I was not sure at first if it was going to be possible to go, but I wanted to see if it was possible. Then everything fell into place. It felt so exciting to get on the plane and land in India.'

Several months later, Sandra returned refreshed and renewed after her journey. She said: 'Now I have a different perspective on life. Now I appreciate and enjoy all that life has to offer. I feel totally happy and at peace with myself after going to India. I also feel a lot stronger in myself. The experience of being in a foreign country on my own, where I had few possessions, made me realize how free I truly was.'

THE THRESHOLD OF CHOICE

If you are coming up to an important choice point, then you are feeling the approach of this threshold. This threshold might be whispering:

- What important choices are you facing right now?
- What important choices are you refusing to face right now?
- What would you rather be doing in your life?
- Where would you love to be doing in life?
- Who would you rather be hanging out with?
- What is calling to you in your life right now?
- What is the first step on this journey?

KNOWING YOUR CORE VALUES

Take a look through the below list, and note the ones that really feel important to you. (Please note: this is not about thinking in terms of *shoulds* or *maybes*; it is about feeling and knowing what is truly important to you.) Now choose your top five and put them in order of priority:

- Abundance, adventure, appreciation, authenticity, achievement;
- Beauty, belonging, bravery;
- Challenge, commitment, compassion, competition, communication, cooperation, creativity, courage, curiosity;
- Diversity, devotion, dynamism, efficiency, empathy, equality, expression;
- Fairness, family, flexibility, flow, freedom, friends, fulfilment, fun;
- Generosity, growth, happiness, harmony, helpfulness, honesty, humour;
- Inspiration, integrity, intelligence, innovation, intuition;
- Joy, keeping agreements;
- Laughter, leadership, learning, logic, love, loyalty;
- Maturity, nobility, non-violence, openness, organizing;
- Passion, peace, people, play, precision, purpose;
- Recognition, reflection, reliability, respect, risk-taking;
- Silence, security, self-discipline, self-expression, self-realization, sensitivity, service, simplicity, spirituality, spontaneity, stability, stimulation;
- Variety, vision, wisdom.

Once you have identified your top five values write a few sentences on each, answering what makes this quality/value so important to you. If you find it hard to really articulate why you find this important, this may be a sign that the value is not really yours. Please note that the answers you give will make sense to you but may not make sense to another person.

TIME TO MOVE ON?

If you think you are standing at a choice point, take a look at some of the following factors:

BURNT OUT – Feeling burnout, stress, overwhelm, or overload are all indicators that you are approaching a choice point;

STUCK – When you feel stuck or unhappy, then pause and ask yourself, Is there any more juice in this situation? If not, it could be time to move on;

OFF-TRACK – If you are doing something to make someone else happy, and you are not on track in your own life, this is another sign of approaching a choice point;

OVER-WORKED — If you are running around trying to multitask and balance too many tasks, then you could reaching a choice point;

UNFULFILLED — Feeling unfulfilled, unrewarded, unfairly treated, frustrated, or joyless indicates that you are at a choice point.

TRAVELLER OF STORMS

O Traveller of storms
Perhaps you can feel
The earth trembling
The sky darkening
Something brews.

Shadows lengthen
Sun descends
Nature stills
Through mist,
Unknown shorelines.

O Traveller of storms
The wise know
When to let go.
Be unattached
To past pleasures,
Or future joys.

In this potent moment
On that lonely edge
Time to embrace
Your bold heart,
And the fierce wave
Sweeping in
Carrying you far away.

— *STEVE AHNAEL NOBEL*

The Threshold of Outer Crisis

If we refuse the choice, or make a reactive or 'bad' choice, we are swept into the threshold of crisis. Not making a choice, or making a bad choice, is just the beginning. (The presuppositions of neurolinguistic programming (NLP) tell us that a person is always making the best choice they can, given their map of the world. That choice may seem self-defeating, odd, or stupid from the outside, but for the person it seems the best way at the time.)

Not making a choice, or making a 'bad' choice, allows the catalyst to enter the fray. This is where the 'fun' really starts. A catalyst is anything or anyone that lights the fuse and blows up our old life. A catalyst can be a tyrant or a lover; a conversation with a friend or stranger; or an event, such as a redundancy, a love affair, an illness, an accident, or some other triggering situation or event.

Although the crisis is triggered by an outer event, there is naturally pain and discomfort. The catalyst is meant to trigger all the build-up of discomfort and pain and release it. This release is difficult, and it is meant to be. Fay said of her catalytic moment: 'I was 28 and going through a catastrophic relationship breakdown. Up to that point, I had succeeded in repressing, running away from, and blocking the truth of the pain in my life. I had used drugs, alcohol, sex, relationships, travelling, to escape the truth. But now I had a daughter and there was nowhere left to run.'

When the catalyst does its job properly, the soul tension is released as the inner and outer structures lose their ability to block the impulse from the soul. Greta was planning to marry and live in the United Kingdom, but as the time got closer, she realized she could not go through with it and went back to her native New Zealand and had to rethink the direction of her life.

The catalyst is not always successful first time around, and they can come in for another run or step aside for another catalyst to finish the job. One woman friend of mine who has been married for many years met a catalyst in the form of a lover while on a spiritual retreat. In many ways, she seemed to have a strong marriage, and there was love and support between the pair. The issue was that she was feeling a pull towards spirituality and her partner was not interested. So a catalyst entered. The affair was intense and brief, but it failed to break through the structures holding her old life in place—the social structures around the marriage were still strong. Although the woman stayed in the marriage, four years later she was still pining over this lost lover and was in danger of meeting another lover to finish off the job.

Another young woman met a catalyst and conceived a child with him. Even though he was emotionally and verbally abusive, she found it hard to let him go. Eventually, when her daughter was 18 months old, she realized that having no father physically present was better than having an abusive father present. Also she realized that letting go of the catalyst could lead to a better-quality masculine energy entering her reality in the future. An important point about lovers as catalysts: they seem very attractive, but under no circumstances consider a catalyst as a long-term prospect. This is a source of great pain for some, yet once the job is done the catalyst will leave. In some cases, it drags on because the catalyst has not completely done the job. This often leaves the recipient in various states of pain, regret, fantasy, and obsessing.

Human life is so varied, and there are many variations on the theme of the catalyst. Sometimes, a number of forces act together to create a breakthrough. I met Jenny in Greece. She was taking time to find herself again after a difficult period. I asked her about her journey, and she told me about her studies at university and then starting work in the hotel business.

She told me: 'I loved the people, but it was hard work. Then the hotel owners asked me to also manage a pub they owned, and this was tough. I had no days off, there was a difficult member of staff to manage, and I was not very much supported.'

Things got tough for Jenny when her boyfriend confessed that he had slept with another woman. She tried to work it through, but decided she could not. She started to have panic attacks and was put on antidepressants for several months. Then she started a new relationship.

'At this point, I went a little bit off the rails, drinking too much, partying, getting hung over, being late for work, and not being my usual responsible self. My family and friends were worried, but no-one said anything to me. Then came the crunch point: my nan died, and I was drunk at her funeral. My dad sat me down and said I should sort my life out. I decided to take some time off work, and fortunately my family supported me.'

Chris worked part time, which allowed him some space and time to build his own business. 'I loved owning and working in my own businesses. I did not realize that I was a workaholic, and I overdid it and burnt out. I had various warning moments, like physical health issues, and I ignored them all and kept going. Then one day, I just could not get out of bed. I simply stopped functioning.'

Simon grew up in a one-parent family living on a council estate, and as a youth he got involved in petty crime, joy riding, and drugs. At the time, Simon identified himself as a kind of Artful Dodger. One big turning point happened while he was committing a burglary in a house: he looked at the picture of the family who owned the house and realized, *I am better than this, and there must be more to my life than robbing houses.* He was arrested some months afterwards and sentenced to six months' imprisonment. This was a turning point in his life.

Damien started his working life as a chartered accountant and was earning a big salary. He worked for a number of different employers, including some of the big international banks in the City of London. He had a habit of moving from contract to contract. He kept climbing the ladder, and each time got a better contract with more money. Damien told me: 'By my 28th birthday, I was feeling that I had pushed my life as far as it would go. Then I had a big wake-up call. I was driving on the M1 motorway, heading north, when I overtook a lorry. I was doing around 100 miles an hour, and the lorry driver did not see me and pulled into my lane. He clipped the back of my car and sent my car into a spin. I was spinning across six lanes, and my whole life actually did flash before my eyes. In those moments, I had the painful thought that I had wasted my life pleasing others and that I had not begun my true work yet. Then I must have passed out, because when I came to on the other side of the motorway, the car was stationary and I was alive, although the car was a write-off. Everything in my life eventually started to unravel after that. My habit of chasing money stopped, and I began a journey that changed everything.'

THE THRESHOLD OF CRISIS

If you feel you could be approaching a threshold of crisis then here are a few questions worth asking yourself:

- Where are you hiding or pretending?
- What are you not willing to notice in your life?
- Where are you holding on?
- What feelings are you not allowing?
- What pain are you avoiding?
- What options or choices are you refusing to face?

Take it moment by moment, and you will find that we are all,
As I've said before, bugs in amber.

— *KURT VONNEGUT*

The Threshold of Inner Crisis

Soul tension leads to a catalyst-crisis, but this one is different—the real crisis happens mostly internally. We have refused the choice, perhaps out of uncertainty or confusion. We may feel distracted by too much happening on the outside. The soul calling is strong, but we cannot translate that into any meaningful response. A catalyst enters the fray and then when the crisis hits the real drama will happen on the inside. When it hits, we are thrown into a super-rough transition. The trigger could be an external event and then we enter into a radical shake-up of our ego structures, our sense of self, our meaning, and our direction/purpose.

Of course, knowing this does not make the journey any easier at this stage. We can deal with the roof being blown off our actual house more easily than handle an internal cracking of the psyche. We cannot call repairmen into the latter as easily as we can the former. This cracking creates an existential crisis, which is allowing 'the creative unknown' to enter our lives. This creative unknown is only realized much further down the path.

An existential crisis can be triggered in a number of ways and I want to briefly discuss three important areas that relate to this threshold.

1. PSYCHEDELICS

There are now a number of psychedelics available that have the potential to trigger an awakening and an existential crisis. Drugs such as ayahuasca, iboga, ecstasy, magic mushrooms, peyote, or LSD have the potential to open us up psychically and spirituality. (Dr. Albert Hoffman, who discovered LSD, believed that it should be used sparingly, as a means to spiritual enlightenment in the same way that peyote was used wisely by American Indians.)

One, in particular, ayahuasca, is mostly used in a spiritual ceremonial context. A few friends experienced this spiritual portal and encouraged me to try it. So, in 2006, I did, and it was by no means a gentle meeting. There were perhaps 40 others taking part in the ayahuasca ceremony. After taking the brew three times, I had strange visions and was taken to dimensions where I faced my deepest fear—that of insanity. My senses felt scrambled, and when I came back I could not remember who I was, who these other people were, or what I was doing in the ceremony. I lost my ability to think.

I had literally lost my mind, and it took me a month to properly recover. The experience felt in some ways like a death of something but the rebirth was still far off, in some distant future. I often wonder if this was the first catalyst for my own super-rough transition, which began in earnest in 2010.

Ayahuasca is a brew of certain plants from the Amazon, which contains the important ingredient of DMT. The psychedelic results of using ayahuasca include visions as well as great elation, fear, or illumination. The Goddess can reveal both the light and the dark in the psyche of the user, whichever is most relevant at the time. There are also great purging properties to the brew. Many who have encountered the Goddess Ayahuasca receive healing and spiritual revelation regarding their true purpose on the earth. The Goddess Ayahuasca commonly grants access to higher-dimensional realms and to spiritual beings who can act as guides or healers in some capacity.

This can be a strong experience, and it is certainly not for the faint-hearted. As far as possible, ensure the credibility of the teacher or group organizing the ceremony. Please note: the legality of using the prepared ayahuasca brew is a grey area. Attitudes and laws change quickly around the Goddess Ayahuasca, so anything I say here may be out of date in a few months. What I can say is that if you feel the call to this particular portal, you should check the current legal status, and if you do go ahead, then it should only be used under the guidance of a trained experienced shaman.

2. SHAMANIC ILLNESS

Shamanism is the oldest spiritual path on the planet, going back some 40,000 years. Mircea Eliade, that great writer on shamanism, calls it a 'technique of ecstasy,' and ecstasy means to be taken out of oneself. A shaman is said to be someone who can journey into the spirit worlds for advice, guidance, help, healing, and power. The call to shamanism is a soul calling, and the shamanic illness that can follow is a result of resistance to the calling.

Spontaneous callings to shamanism can appear at any age and can be heralded by: uncommon dreams, visions, the feeling that unseen beings are around, a need to withdraw and spend time alone, depression, and a strong desire to be in nature. Traditionally, it was believed that you do not choose this path; the path chooses you. The catalyst that begins the journey can be external, such as a near-death experience, but often the soul tension simply reaches a point where the physical-emotional-mental structures start to break down and accident or illness results.

The calling can happen in the industrialized West just as easily as it does in tribal regions of the world. Of course, in the West, this calling is often not recognized for what it truly is. This path is challenging (which is why many refuse the calling), but to refuse can lead to shamanic illness.

Mircea Eliade describes the shamanic calling in a traditional tribal context: 'In Siberia, the youth who is called to be a shaman attracts attention by his strange behaviour; for example, he seeks solitude, becomes absentminded, loves to roam in the woods or unfrequented places, has visions, and sings in his sleep.'

Traditionally, the call of the spirits leads the initiate to a psychological and spiritual trial, where he or she dies to their former self. Janet StraightArrow, an American shamanic practitioner, has this to say about the calling: 'A Shaman remembers the knowledge in their bones of truth, beauty, health, happiness, and light. Some of the work is seen in the world, but most of it is in the unseen. A Shaman who does not answer the call to action or one who acts outside of natural and cosmic laws may pay the price in unhappiness, illness, and even death.' In the West, we do not understand shamanic calling or shamanic illness. A friend of mine, Molly, hit a crisis when she was 41 years of age, just past her Uranus Opposition. She attended a workshop on creative writing and had a personal breakthrough. The facilitator was talking about the difference between dreams and fantasy, and in that moment, she realized how much she had used daydreaming in her life as a coping strategy. This was both upsetting and also a great realization for her.

For the next few weeks, she became mindful of the times she slipped into fantasy. She sat with it and found that underneath all the fantasizing was a tremendous amount of anger and grief. There were also feelings of disconnection, loneliness, emptiness. and the sense of being an outsider. Not long afterwards, during a different workshop, she experienced a manic episode during which she felt hyper, spaced out, and could not eat or sleep. She felt vulnerable and out of control. There was also a great sense of meaninglessness, as if nothing in her past life mattered.

She sought medical help and, for a time, was put on anti-psychotic medication. We met up whilst she was still on medication and going through her crisis phase. Sometimes, the calling is just as dramatic but less crazy making. During my transition, I interviewed a fellow author, Richard, for a podcast series. I asked him what set him off on his mystical journey of awakening, and he told me that it began in his twenties, when he fell asleep in a wood. When he awoke, he found that he was surrounded by adder snakes that just lay and watched him for almost an hour before moving off. This was a powerful shamanic turning point in Richard's life, which later opened him to series of deep insights into the human condition.

3. KUNDALINI AWAKENING

A kundalini awakening can be triggered by all manner of catalysts, but usually it erupts via some intense spiritual practice. In Sanskrit, the word *kundalini* translates as 'coiled,' and it is usually described as a 'sleeping coiled serpent.' It is also sometimes called 'Serpent Power,' and it is a force of tough love that is said to be located at the base of the spine between the root and sacral chakras. It remains dormant until awakened by spiritual practice.

One woman who was having a spontaneous kundalini experience in a tantra workshop said,'I began to scream, and I kept screaming… . I was utterly out of control, my body wracked with wave after wave of energy.'

My own super-rough transition was via a beautiful Texan woman called Lisa who sparked a kundalini experience in me. We had met 18 months previously and become friends. Then, in January 2010, Lisa organized a workshop for me in Ireland. The night before the workshop, I had a strange and powerful dream in which we were married by angels. I awoke with the image of Lisa smiling at me, all dressed in white. I did not the take the dream too seriously, and when I met Lisa for breakfast I told her about the dream. She listened in silence and said nothing.

I quickly dismissed the dream, and shortly afterwards, we went for a walk along the Waterford coastline with some friends. After a brisk walk, I stood for a few minutes with Lisa, looking out over a calm sea. We stood in silence and watched as a speedboat raced along the coastline heading our way. As it passed, an adult male voice shouted our way, 'Just say yes!' I had no idea what he was talking about until a friend came up to us, laughing and saying that the stranger thought I was proposing to Lisa.

After the workshop was over, I returned to England. About a week later, I chatted with Lisa over Skype. It was then that Lisa confessed that she really liked me. Without even thinking, I replied that I really liked her, too. Within a short few weeks, we were engaged in a long-distance passionate affair over Skype. Although nothing physically was happening, psychically all sorts of stuff was going on. Because of the intensity and sexual chemistry being stirred up, I knew I was heading into very choppy waters. But I could also feel a soul calling that was hard to ignore.

Then, for me. came the defining moment. I suggested that we do a tantric meditation together over Skype. We did the exercise for about 15 minutes, and when we stopped I could feel pulsating waves of energy in my body unlike anything I had ever felt before. We said our goodnights, and I went to bed, but as I lay awake I felt strange, my limbs were shaking, and there were these odd ripples or tremors of energy flowing up my body. I had never experienced anything quite like this, and although it all sounds mystical and wonderful, the actual experience was more like being in the midst of some mild internal electric storm.

I just lay there feeling wave after wave of energy flowing through me, and it seemed to go on for hours, until I eventually fell asleep. In the days, weeks, and months ahead, the intensity of the experience faded, but never completely. Right up until the early stages of renewal. I could feel the energy humming away in the background. In the stages up until then, sometimes the waves would grow in intensity and then all I could do then was rest as the waves pulsed through me.

During this time, I sat down and had a heart-to-heart chat with my partner, Ursula. To cut a long story short, she agreed to let me explore this connection, and I went to Ireland. We spent five intimate days by the sea in Galway. Meeting Lisa felt like I was meeting a part of myself—one that was living at a level of freedom I had long forgotten. When we talked or sat in silence, what I noticed were qualities I felt I had yet to fully awaken. I loved her warmth, her courage, her sense of adventure, and her love of play and creativity. I could feel then that she was a mirror of sorts, pointing the way to a new life.

What I did not realize at the time was how this love affair would eventually burn away and destroy my old life. The catalyst Lisa had introduced me to the catalytic kundalini experience (and just for the record, I want to state that the energy waves are still with me, although in a gentler form, as I enter the new year of 2014).

The kundalini experience can be consciously induced by a number of practices, such as hatha yoga postures, *pranayama* or breathwork, intense meditation, or by working with sound and sacred mantras. (As mentioned, in my own case it was activated by tantric meditation.) The book *Kundalini: Path to Higher Consciousness* by Gopi Krishna has a beautiful description of the kundalini awakening experience:

Suddenly, with a roar like that of a waterfall, I felt a stream of liquid light entering my brain through the spinal cord. Entirely unprepared for such a development, I was completely taken by surprise.... The illumination grew brighter and brighter, the roaring louder. I experienced a rocking sensation and then felt myself slipping out of my body, entirely enveloped in a halo of light. It is impossible to describe the experience accurately. I felt the point of consciousness that was myself growing wider surrounded by waves of light.

It is said that the Goddess Kundalini cannot be rushed, and that it is imperative to be prepared; otherwise, it can be like running too much electrical current through a weak circuit. I once met a man who had engaged in a committed Buddhist practice for many years. Then he went to see an acupuncturist to help with a physical problem, and when the first needle was inserted it triggered an explosion of energy. The man had a few sessions, and each one had the same effect. He began to have these explosions outside of the sessions. He would inexplicably laugh and loudly 'roar' in all manner of situations. From this time onwards, he could no longer meditate. He is still integrating the experience some years on.

When the kundalini current manages to rise through all the chakras, it is said that it has the power to expel the darkness of the past, unknot any traumas caught in the memory of the body, free the person from the karma of past lives, and also clear present-life traumas.

THE GODDESS KUNDALINI

Kundalini energy is a force that is raw, vital, and powerful, and thus is to be respected. When such an awakening happens, the layers of our everyday personality can be swept away suddenly. Signs and symptoms of kundalini awakening include:

- Involuntary shaking in the body;
- Sensations of heat in the spine,
- Intense experiences of inner colour and light;
- Internal waves or bolts of energy,
- Sensitivity to light, sound, and touch;
- Headaches, migraines, or pressure inside the skull;
- Pains in the head and back of the neck;
- Anxiety, confusion, or uncertainty about what is happening;
- Strong emotional shifts or extreme mood swings;
- Greatly diminished or increased sexual desire;
- Precognition, knowing about events or synchronicities before they happen;
- Intense bliss followed by acute pain;
- Transcendent awareness and feelings of infinite love.

SHAMANIC ILLNESS

When the spirits start to connect, it can feel like our psychic defences are being pulled down, and then we may seek to withdraw or find solace in alternative pursuits such as yoga or meditation. Also wild places may feel comforting in a strange way. We may start to feel the call of the spirits in ways that feel frightening at first. Confusion and depression may result. The call is there, but the conscious mind has no idea what to do with it. There can be visions and sensitivity to too much sensory input.

The calling wants to break through our ego filters to help us see, hear, feel, smell, and taste the universe in more direct ways. If successful, this will put us in touch with a magical and primal universe. Here, we find the universe filled with elemental spirits, spirit guides, and deep ancestral sources of healing.

In shamanic societies, the shamanic calling and symptoms are usually recognized quickly and the individual is taken under the wing of an experienced practitioner. In the industrialized West, the individual may be diagnosed as suffering from mental illness. (Of course, the shamanic calling is not the only cause of mental illness.) From personal experience, and from helping some close friends, I would say that shamanic illness cannot be treated in a conventional way. Although drugs may suppress the symptoms, real healing only happens when the calling is recognized and embraced.

THE GODDESS AYAHUASCA

Ayahuasca, commonly called vine of the dead, is a brew made for divinatory, healing and spiritual revelation purposes by the native peoples of Peru. Ayahuasca is made to be taken in sacred ceremony. People who have taken ayahuasca speak of massive spiritual revelations regarding their true purpose, and the nature of all life on earth. Ayahuasca has great purging qualities. The Goddess Ayahuasca seeks to wake us up to a new level of consciousness and many describe this form of spiritual awakening as a kind of death and rebirth. The Goddess Ayahuasca gives individuals access to spiritual dimensions and opens up contact with various other dimensional beings who can act as guide, healer, or teacher. When we are opened up in this way we may start to experience time in different ways such as seeing along timelines into the future. We may visit other dimensions of reality and visit other civilisations. We may be taken through the portal of our death or be brought face to face with our deepest fear. The visions of the Goddess Ayahuasca can be tremendously beautiful and light as well as very terrifying and dark.

It's possible I am pushing through solid rock
in flint like layers, as the ore lies, alone.
I am such a long way in I see no way through…

—*RAINER MARIA RILKE*

The Dark Night Experience

A super-rough transition can include what has been called a 'dark night of the soul' experience. Here, nothing makes sense in the same way anymore, and there is a loss of meaning or driving purpose and a great sense of isolation and alienation. The dark night is the death of the illusionary self, the collapse of old limiting ego structures, which can feel like the collapse of a building, leaving us feeling lost and homeless for a time. It can also feel like the collapse of a bridging structure, leaving us feeling stranded on one side of a ravine, unsure how to cross over to the other side.

This is a form of suffering like no other. The experience seems to thwart our will or resources at every turn. The catalyst here can be a psychologically challenging or traumatic event, such as a major loss, a life-threatening experience, or a reaction to using a recreational drug. Whatever the cause, there is a major shattering of current reality and our ego-body consciousness struggles to make sense or meaning out of experience. There will also be difficulty in navigating many everyday challenges, such as work or relationships.

One of my friends, Joni, is a filmmaker who went to Bali in her early twenties to study under a spiritual teacher. Under his guidance, she had a catalytic experience in a cave in a forest where she meditated blindfolded for several hours. This experience opened her up to a state of peace and wonder. When she emerged from the cave, she saw light everywhere and experienced life as being 'an interconnected web of prana.'

She returned to England after three weeks, and coming back was disorientating. It was not long before she ran out of money, and after a child-minding job ended after several months, she eventually became homeless. She descended into a dark time, as she stayed in a youth hostel, which increased her sense of vulnerability and isolation. She later told me, 'It took me around three years to get back on my feet.'

Jasmine had been married for nine years and had a young child when she met Alex. They met through mutual friends and discovered they lived close to each other, had similar lifestyles, and most importantly, had a shared spiritual outlook. Although nothing really romantic happened between them, it did create an emotional explosion in Jasmine's life. After one of their meetups, Alex walked Jasmine to her car and confessed to her that he felt there was 'an energy' between them. Jasmine agreed, and now they both knew they were sailing into tricky waters.

Although there had been no physical intimacy, not long afterwards Jasmine experienced a kundalini awakening. She told me, 'I felt a massive surge of energy that affected my whole body. It felt wonderfully orgasmic, which left me shaking for days.' The experience quietened down but continued in the background for some months.

As the tension was building between them, they decided to speak openly with their partners. Alex's wife 'went mad' and directed her anger at Jasmine, as Alex distanced himself with no real explanation. Jasmine told me: 'The lack of communication left me worrying that he thought I was unworthy of spending time with him. I initially accepted Alex's wife's interpretation of me, and started to see myself as some horrible person who wanted to sabotage their relationship. I felt such deep despair and anger that was tempered by a longing for his love. It was such a difficult and confusing time, and it nearly sent me crazy. Soon after, I fell into a dark night of the soul experience, where I judged and doubted myself. The dark night seemed to last forever.'

The dark night experience, when it arises, is not limited to this stage alone; in many cases, it continues into the following stage of release, and even further into recalibration. There is advice in Chapter Two about crossing the emotional abyss, and also more advice in the chapters ahead. For now, here is some basic advice for the dark night experience.

THE DARK NIGHT

When confronted by a dark night experience consider this simple advice:

- Very importantly, practise being gentle and compassionate with yourself;
- Following as a close second is patience. Sometimes, doing nothing is the best thing. Patience helps with relaxation;
- The next important thing to do is surrender, which might not come immediately. Just reflect on the fact that you are entering a powerful time of incubation, initiation, fallowness, and hibernation;

- Learn to handle stress more effectively. Embrace activities and people that nurture and support you and say 'no' to anything that taxes you or affects you negatively;
- Isolation is a major issue, so stay in touch with your support network. Although you want to hibernate, it is useful to stay connected to the outside world;
- Honour when you need to be alone, and do not force yourself into busyness;
- Journal your dreams, thoughts, and feelings—taking 'dark' thoughts or visions out of your head and onto paper can be very healing;
- Stay focused on maintaining an uplifted state. This can be done through playing gentle ambient music, reading an inspiring book, watching a hopeful movie. or visiting places that uplift your spirit. such as a beautiful café or garden;
- Get a physical check-up with your physician, but also consider including other alternative approaches, such as psychotherapy, gentle massage, acupuncture, or energy healing.

8

Rain and Wax

The Greek myth of the minotaur begins as Daedalus the architect is forced into exile from his native Athens with his son Icarus. He finds work as an architect in Crete and is soon set to work building the famous labyrinth that housed the infamous creature. The hero Theseus, with the help of the Princess Ariadne, manages to kill the minotaur, escape the labyrinth, and flee Crete by boat before the king of Crete can do anything about it. The king suspects Daedalus of helping the pair and imprisons father and son in a high tower. Daedalus knows that escape by sea is perilous since the king's fleet is now on high alert, so he decides to escape by air and builds two sets of wings out of wax, reeds, and feathers. Giving one pair to his son, he cautions him not to fly too close to the sun or too close to the water—the former would cause the wax to melt and the latter would dampen the wings and weigh them down. With this warning in mind, the two leap out into the air and are soon soaring high above the glittering ocean... .

* * *

Now the transition begins in earnest, as soul tension breaks through all resistance and dissolves our life, like dew in the rising sun. However, when the experience is tougher, it is like iron ore in a burning hot furnace. The more we try to hold onto the old life, the faster it seems to fly off and disappear.

Endings happen when lovers, marriage partners, friends, family members, business partners, or work colleagues just up and go. Sometimes, this can feel like a gradual letting go, and sometimes, it is quite sudden. People enter our lives for a moment, others for a season; a few stay around for a whole lifetime. This can be disconcerting and painful when it happens too quickly, or when too many things leave at the same time.

When my transition hit, not only did lover and career go but also a couple of close, supportive friends decided to leave without so much as a farewell. Endings are not limited to people leaving; endings also mean disintegration, where old supporting structures start to melt away. Everything is energy, and every structure is held in place by an energetic blueprint. When your existing blueprint dissolves, so too do the structures of your life start to wobble and break down.

Work is one energy structure, relationships another, and home another. People come together through the connection of shared values, interests, and love. When the underlying energy of these bonds weakens or dissolves, then there is no longer any real reason to hang out together. A relationship that once felt alive and vibrant no longer feels the same way. Our passion or sense of purpose around our work can dissolve, leaving us devoid of any meaningful direction. When it is time to let go, we are not just letting go of some outer thing like a house or a relationship; we are also letting go of the hopes and expectations attached to them. This makes the letting go all the harder.

In this phase, our attachment to our possessions can shift, and even disappear. Just as importantly, endings are about psychological change. This is the other side of the coin, so to speak. Our inner sense of self is built up over time and shifts with the various developmental stages, as outlined in Chapter Two. Release clears out any limiting notions that tell us our future is a reflection of our past. When we drop such limiting ideas, the future can be created afresh.

To let go is to release the images and emotions, the grudges and fears, the clinging and disappointments of the past that bind our spirit.
— *JACK KORNFIELD*

The Way of Smooth Release

In a smooth transition, soul tension builds to the point where we choose to leave. Like Daedalus and Icarus, we make good our escape from a difficult past and we take the leap of freedom and trust that the wind will carry us onwards and upwards. Sometimes, it is not a question of leaving something; rather, it is about stepping directly into something new. In either case, we feel something important is missing in our lives. Perhaps we want more adventure, fun, fulfilment, intimacy, laughter, or love in our lives. Perhaps the old life does not fulfil us anymore. Or perhaps we are waiting for something to come along and entice us forward into a new phase. Whichever way we go, it can mean saying goodbye to an existing way of life, whether it be home, relationship, friends, or job.

A smooth release is not usually emotionally challenging in the way a rough or super-rough release can be. However, even positive endings can bring up feelings as poet, journalist, and novelist Anatole France comments, 'All changes, even the most longed for, have their melancholy; for what we leave behind us is a part of ourselves; we must die to one life before we can enter another.'

Here, we are more likely to take positive action to help accelerate the ending. Sita felt she was coming to the end of a cycle. When she reflected on her life, she felt a pressing desire for change but she also saw her resistance to change.

She told me: 'I felt stuck and unhappy, so I went to San Diego for a month and did a 30-day kundalini yoga course that included daily sound healing and massage. I deliberately went into this process to work on releasing my attachments. Every morning, I would write positive affirmations for my life and place them under my yoga mat. I also asked for help and divine guidance in removing energy blocks from my life, relationships, and direction. When I was there I did not think I shifted or changed in any way, but when I got home I realized that two of my major energy blocks were not there anymore. This enabled me to pass through a rite of passage that previously I had been unable to tread. I felt liberated in my energy field and in my external reality. Some things left my life, and this helped open up the space.'

Transitions are about relationships, and endings help to shake them up. If a relationship has become dull, painful, or abusive, then leaving may eventually become the only option.

Vena says: 'It took me two years to make the decision to complete my marriage. It became apparent that I could either choose to stay in the marriage and slowly die inside, or I could get a divorce. In February 2005, I chose the divorce. The year that followed was a roller-coaster of both deep grief and real exhilaration, but I came home to myself in a way that I never had before.'

Often, we resist ending a relationship, even when it has become abusive. In 2012, when I was in Greece on holiday, I met Karina, who turned out to be a real-life Shirley Valentine.

Karina told me: 'By the time I got up the resources and courage to leave my abusive relationship, most of my friends had grown tired and left me, too. An astrologer told me Greece would be a good place for me. For a time I wasn't able to pull it off financially, and so I let the dream go. Four years went by until I started to feel "if not now, when?" So I quit my job and left. For me, leaving, I had no grief only joy and, of course. the fear of how I was going to do it all and travel with a child alone. I didn't miss home; in fact, my heart felt more at home in Greece. I am still in transition, which is a tricky place to be, but I did something huge by quitting my job and going to Greece. Now my concept of what is totally possible in my life has changed and hugely expanded. I'm happy I made the change to end a decision, but if one person approaches the ending consciously, then it can make all the difference.'

Sometimes, both individuals make the choice to leave together. Abramović and Ulay were together for a decade, and they agreed to take a pilgrimage to end their relationship. They had the idea of each of walking the Great Wall of China but from different ends. Ulay started from the Gobi Desert and Abramović from the Yellow Sea, and they each walked around 2,500 km before meeting in the middle to say good-bye. It was the end of a relationship full of 'mysticism, energy, and attraction.'

Sometimes, the period of ending is not sudden or clear cut. Endings very commonly affect our work. Mary was still in her old job but felt she had energetically left several months before. The organization she worked for had gone through an aborted merger and subsequently entered into a period of restructuring. She felt disconnected and drifting while the organization went through its own process of change. She was eventually offered redundancy after a long period of uncertainty. Sometimes, the ending is more graceful. When Glenn had a transition during his Chiron Return, he was able to quickly negotiate a good package to leave his career in law, giving him the space and resources to follow his passion for spirituality and service.

Endings impact our inner world, our sense of self, and how we see the world. It is not only emotions that shift at this time; beliefs and values are also coming to the surface to be evaluated. Spanish poet Antonio Machado once wrote, 'Under all that we think lives all we believe, like the ultimate veil of our spirits.' Beliefs are self-fulfilling prophecies—they are the invisible limits we place on our ability, capacity, flexibility, and resourcefulness.

A smooth release happens because we are moving towards a more compelling future, and this gives us more impetus to bust through any limiting beliefs standing in the way. Desire and expectation creates a certain unstoppable momentum. Anyone who has moved towards a goal or dream outside their comfort zone will tell you that realizing the goal shifts something on the inside. Before my last but one transition, I did some workshops and ongoing trainings that helped me get clear on my dreams and goals and then focus some energy into realizing them. This led me into a new reality as a company director, public speaker, and published author. I also created a loving and stable long-term relationship. As a result of this, my beliefs around what I was capable of achieving shifted for good.

Alongside belief comes our values, and these also shift in a transition. Our values determine our behaviour and choices. A transition can often help us to understand our core values and release the values of others. It is not uncommon to take on the values of parents in the mistaken belief that they are our own. Perhaps, we rebel against our parents' values to find a separate sense of self. Rebelling against our parents does not mean that we find a truer sense of self; it can lead us to feel just as confused and lost. This is perhaps one of the greatest gifts of transition: it returns us to the earthing ground of authenticity. This shifting of belief and values begins in release and continues well towards the end of the transition journey.

Most importantly, release is a two-way activity. Yes, people, possessions, and situations can up and leave, but we are participants in the journey and we must learn that sometimes we need to consciously let go. Letting go is not about forgetting, or shutting down, or trying to block something or someone. It isn't about losing or giving up. Letting go is the opposite of trying to control or force a situation. Ultimately, letting go is an act of self-compassion. It allows us and others the space to move on. Letting go is about freedom, hence the old Zen proverb, 'Let go or be dragged.'

Personally, I believe it is a good practice to at least once in our lives experience letting go of our material possessions. This I have found to be a real test of attachment. Nothing is ours to keep; we are merely stewards of material possessions for a time. I would say a good rule of thumb, in general, is to only keep things that are really useful or that you really love. There is no point keeping things that remind you by association of an outgoing phase of life. This will keep you tied energetically to the past in some way. In any case, a transition is a time when life is more volatile, and having too many possessions can feel burdensome. Of course, whether you put stuff into storage or give it away is a matter of preference.

In my life, I have given away most of my possessions twice, both times during a transition. These experiences brought me much lightness and relief and taught me I am not defined by what I own. In all transition, the old rule that nature abhors a vacuum applies, and it is amazing how quickly new possessions can be attracted back into our lives.

This principle also applies to people. As author Paolo Coelho says, 'When someone leaves, it's because someone else is about to arrive.' For this reason alone, learning to cut 'the ties that bind' is an essential practice to free us up for our future life. Letting go is as much an energetic practice as it is a practical one. (I recommend the book *Cutting the Ties That Bind* by Phyllis Krystal.)

RITUAL OF RELEASE

1. Take a walk in nature and find some pebbles for this ritual. Dark or black pebbles seem to work well for releasing. Take one of these pebbles and bring a thought, feeling, person, or situation to mind that you want to release. Take a moment to dwell on this and then blow the energy of the thought, person, or situation into the stone.

2. Then release the pebble to nature—perhaps, by throwing it into a lake— and ask that the old energy be released back to the elements. For a person or situation, ask that all involved be released to their highest destiny.

3. Since nature abhors a vacuum, to finish choose another pebble as a means of inviting something new into your life. Lighter or white pebbles seem to work well for this. Find the feeling of the new thought, person, or situation, and in the same way, blow your intention into the pebble and release it to nature. You can repeat this a number of times with different qualities or new experiences you want to slowly but surely enter your life.

> *This being human is a guest house.*
> *Every morning is a new arrival.*
> *A joy, a depression, a meanness,*
> *Some momentary awareness*
> *comes as an unexpected visitor…*
> *Welcome and entertain them all.*
> — *RUMI*

The Way of Rough Release

In the classical version of the Greek myth, Daedalus and Icarus make good their escape, and flying high they soar past the Greek islands of Samos, Delos, and Lebynthos. Then Icarus suddenly soars upwards into the heavens, where the blazing sun melts the wax holding his wings together. In a rough release, we are Daedalus, watching helplessly as Icarus spirals down to his death. (This sea became known forever after as the Icarian Sea.) We are distraught and lost, not knowing what to do next. Rough release feels intense, humiliating, and dramatic—a form of sudden exile during which we are confronted with a sharp loss of the familiar.

In a rough release, we may feel our life is dissolving as old supporting structures unexpectedly and suddenly fall away. Perhaps, we did not consciously want them to go. Friends and lovers may leave, or a business partnership may come to an end. Unexpected endings are rarely easy, because there is always a certain amount of emotional turbulence, numbness, and confusion. We cannot go back, but the way ahead is not clear. We are not sure what to think or do in the evolving circumstances. We may feel we are oscillating between a known past, an anxious present, and an unknown future. Pain, grief, and confusion come with the territory between something leaving and something new entering our lives.

In a rough transition, there is no desirable goal: we have just the journey and an unknown destination. In many ways, the inner journey is more dramatic and powerful. Because of the intensity and suddenness of the experience, core limiting beliefs can dissolve quickly as internal ego structures shift or collapse. This creates an uncomfortable void where we can feel lost or disorientated for a time (which is only resolved in the next two stages). Similarly, in a rough or super-rough transition, there is usually a powerful shift in values. To value something is to place a high importance on it. Our values determine our direction in life. A transition can lead us into a loss of meaning where our values and priorities shift away and then towards something new. This shift in values is not always understood immediately by the person in the transition process. It can be definitely misunderstood by others. A classic response to someone in transition would be, 'You are not the man or woman I married!'

Values are the building blocks of character, and as the Greek philosopher Heraclitus said, 'A man's character is his guardian divinity.' When we are clear on our values, we will be clear on our direction and purpose in life. With the shift in beliefs and values eventually comes a new sense of self. Naturally, our old sense of self does not leave easily. One of the major signs that our old sense of identity is leaving is confusion. One woman said to me during this phase of her transition, 'If I am not a mother anymore, then who am I?'

This is a process that continues and deepens in the next phase. In my own transition, I felt my old identity wobble to the point that I did not know who I was anymore. Because of this slow shift in beliefs, values, and identity, there can open up a painful void, and we are just as likely to resist the transition here as in the stage of soul tension.

Sometimes, we resist really letting go by trying to re-create the old situation in different forms. For example: It was no secret amongst James's friends that after a long-term relationship broke down he had become a serial monogamist. He found the ending difficult, and so he created profiles on several dating sites and would go through one date after another looking for love again. He was advised by some close friends to slow down and enjoy the time being on his own. Although he could see the wisdom in this in practice, he found it hard to do. After three months of intensive dating (where some weeks he met up with four different dates), he decided to take it easier. Further into the transition, he became more interested in meditation, walking in nature, and spending time away from the world in silence. Through slowing down and not chasing a relationship, his ideas and experience of love changed … but that is a whole different story.

The phase of soul tension can seem to go on for ages and then the phase of release can happen suddenly. Frances lived in a spiritual community for nine 'long arduous years.' She was involved in Buddhist spiritual practice and wanted to become fully part of a local community. An opportunity came up to join an all-female house, and she was accepted. The experience was not what she expected it would be.

'It was awful from the beginning. Within just the first week, I felt I had to make myself small to be there. On the surface, there were rules around spiritual practice, men entering the house, and complex dietary issues. Beneath the surface, there were many unspoken rules and strong group dynamics going on. I felt little emotional connection with the people there, and I often felt hated by others, which left me feeling continual distress. Then came a big eruption, and so I decided to hand in my notice to quit and move out. Two friends in the community decided to move out with me, and we all agreed to find and share a place together. Then, out of the blue, suddenly, these two friends decided that they could not live with me, which was a great shock. I felt betrayed and confused, with no real sense of where I belonged.'

When the release phase happens, it can bring up feelings of shock, vulnerability, and fear. Rabea married and lived with her partner in Berlin. They bought a holiday home in Poland and on the surface lived a perfect life. She qualified as an herbalist and naturopath and loved the work she was doing. Then her partner found a lover, and they divorced in 2011. Rabea told me: 'It was all very painful. At times, I felt like I was dying. Up until this point, my whole life was planned out in my head. I started thinking about having a family. I even started planning the details of where I would conceive in the house. In the relationship, he was very dreamy and floating. I took on the role of being more controlling and responsible. Then, after the separation, I felt like a baby. I did not know who I was anymore, and it was hard to stay connected to my body. At first, when my husband moved out I hoped he would come back. I was so scared to be alone. There was so much grief that came up. I started bodywork and psychotherapy to help me let go of my marriage, my house, and eventually, this led me to a new career as a naturopath.'

There are many ways we can meet a sudden ending—being let go from a job is one. Even in this more enlightened age of work, we read stories of individuals being taken to a supervisor's office and told that this is the end of the line and they should collect their belongings, hand in their keys and passes, and vacate forthwith. Jack was called into the human resources office one afternoon and told he was no longer needed by his company. He had just enough time to say his goodbyes before he was out the door. All his expectations came crashing down, and Jack broke down and just cried in the car park.

Loss is one of the hardest aspects of the human condition. The American writer Henry Miller once said on the subject: 'Life moves on, whether we act as cowards or heroes. Life has no other discipline to impose, if we would but realize it, than to accept life unquestioningly. Everything we shut our eyes to, everything we run away from, everything we deny, denigrate or despise, serves to defeat us in the end.'

THE FIVE STAGES OF GRIEVING

In her book, *On Death and Dying,* Elisabeth Kubler-Ross outlined five stages of loss: denial, anger, bargaining, depression, and acceptance.

DENIAL – The first stage, of denial, helps us to survive the loss. Life makes little sense. There is a conscious or unconscious denial of reality. Often, there is shock, denial, and we feel numb. Denial can be useful insofaras it helps slow down the grieving process and gives space to handle difficult feelings.

ANGER – Anger brings us out of denial. It is important to feel our anger, even though it seems endless. Feeling anger allows old stuck energy to dissipate and flow in new ways. Anger also helps to reveal hidden pain. It is okay to feel angry with yourself or other people. It is okay to feel alone, betrayed, deserted, or abandoned. This stage is about feeling and witnessing rather than reacting.

BARGAINING – We want our old life back; we want things to be the way they were. We reflect back with guilt and regret. What if we had done things differently? What if the illness had been found sooner? What if that person had decided to stay? We think about the past and re-run different scenarios. We may even try to bargain with the pain, or with God, but to no avail.

DEPRESSION – We withdraw from the world and feel that life cannot go on. Depression is a dress rehearsal for the coming 'aftermath' of grief. It's natural to feel sadness, regret, fear, and uncertainty when going through this stage. Depression is a necessary step along the way to fully feeling grief.

ACCEPTANCE – Now we can accept the reality that our old life has left. We may not like it, but we are learning to live with it. We are now grieving for the people or circumstances we have lost, but we also know we need to get on with our life. Feeling grief is the final stage of letting go.

> *Never regret thy fall,*
> *O Icarus of the fearless flight*
> *For the greatest tragedy of them all*
> *Is never to feel the burning light."*
> — OSCAR WILDE

The Way of Super-Rough Release

As we step into a super-rough release we move into an existential crisis, which is where the hard shell of the ego-body consciousness is cracked wide open. We are Icarus plunging out of control to our death in the waiting sea below. We experience an existential death, and our personality is thrown into freefall.

There can be a traumatic experience, such as a lover leaving, the sudden loss of a dear one, a life-threatening situation, which leads to a sense of overwhelm, depression, or an inability to cope with life in the same way. We can feel alone in the world, experience a void of meaning, or be confronted by the shocking realization of our mortality. Our old life is falling away, and this can trigger a sense of disbelief for a time. There can be a feeling of shock, leaving us feeling like a broken pane of glass scattered across the floor. The scattered shards of glass can never be put back together in the same way, no matter how hard we try. This leaves us feeling broken, fragile, and vulnerable in the world. We can be disturbed more easily, and we feel anxious. This shattering can be triggered by an intense spiritual practice, such as prayer, yoga, breathing exercises, chanting, silence, vision questing, meditation, intention, and creative visualization.

This is what happened to Elisabeth. She was passionate about chanting, and sometimes she would do this for hours. This went on for some months, until a psychotic episode erupted, during which she could not tell ordinary reality from 'non-ordinary reality.' I was present when the episode began and witnessed much anxiety and tears. Sometimes, she would cry for hours each day. The most intense part lasted about a week, after which it lessened and she was able to ground herself by walking everyday in nature and surrounding herself with understanding friends and family. She also stopped chanting until she was fully recovered. This episode led to a dramatic release of her old life—friends, home, possessions, and her identity. (I was also witness to her renewal, which was a magical and explorative time. She went travelling and did things she had wanted to do but never had the courage.)

This phase can be deceptive. It can feel initially very light and ecstatic, before becoming more bleak or 'dark.' We can experience unity consciousness and the oneness of creation before hitting something else that often includes a loss of meaning with our current life. The light state does not hold for very long—weeks, perhaps months at most, before opening up to a 'darker' doorway of despair, deep depression, and other inner demons.

Sam describes himself as an ex-serial drug addict, meaning he was not addicted to anything in particular; he just spent a couple of decades taking any recreational drugs. He started smoking marijuana and hashish and soon progressed to LSD. At university, he experimented with cocaine, ecstasy, heroin, and was a regular user of marijuana.

Sam told me: 'When I was younger, I would go to parties. Some of the photos of those times show me resembling a ghost. I did feel dead, and in many ways, drug taking gave me the feeling of dying beautifully. It was too beautiful and also too damaging. When I found ecstasy, I felt a whole world of love and consciousness opening up. I felt regularly at one with whole tribes of ravers. When I was 38, doctors told me I had Hepatitis C. The news was shocking and I instantly stopped all alcohol and drugs. The doctors were not sure if the disease could be passed on sexually, and this affected my relationship with my partner, and within six months she left me. I found myself living in a house with hardly any furniture, and six months later I went bankrupt. With no alcohol or drugs to numb my feelings, I spent many months waking up feeling sick. I would just go through each day feeling very dark, heavy, and depressed.'

Both the experience of taking drugs and the aftermath of darkness and depression led Sam on a journey of self-inquiry, during which time his whole life changed.

A super-rough release can represent a shamanic calling, leading to a shamanic-type illness. Tanya decided to go backpacking around Asia in the summer of 2007. She signed up for a diving course. Her first dive with an instructor was tricky, with lots of manoeuvring around and between rocks and through lots of jellyfish. After this dive, she had the sense not to dive again with the same instructor, but for some reason, she went against this intuition and dived.

'On this dive, something went horribly wrong, I lost consciousness under water, and when I came to, I did not know what was happening. Somehow, I managed to swim up to the surface, but everything seemed different, darker somehow. I felt unwell, but the instructor insisted that everything was fine. I later realized I was suffering from decompression sickness. I started to feel really ill: I felt anxious, edgy, and irritable for no reason, and I could not concentrate or focus. I had no energy, and eventually, my body just crashed. I could no longer work, I could no longer exercise, and my family tried to be helpful but did not know what to do. Most of my friends, not understanding what was going on, left me. I felt isolated, alone, and in despair.'

This experience turned Tanya's life upside down. After a very difficult time, it did lead her to explore different forms of healing, including spending several months in Brazil in a spiritual community with the renowned healer John of God. (In renewal, she went on to train as a healer herself.) However you enter this threshold, whether by the light or dark route, this is still a difficult and intense experience.

In the West, we do not really understand such existential experiences. We are too rational and still too entrenched in mechanistic medical models. Our religious frameworks struggle to comprehend spiritual emergence, which is surprising since Christianity has many examples of saints who have passed through the 'dark night' experience. Psychiatry and psychology make no real distinction between mysticism and mental illness, and because of a lack of supportive psycho-spiritual and practical structures, spiritual emergence can easily turn into spiritual emergency.

In the East, it is very different, from the Indian systems of ayurveda and yoga, to the Buddhist practices of Japan and Tibet, to the shamans of Mongolia and Siberia, there are philosophical frameworks that support the integration of intense spiritual experiences into normal life. When ego structures collapse this creates a crisis of vibration, since heavy emotions are released, and we are for a time dragged down into lower emotional and mental bandwidths. The important thing to remember is that this is a time of release, and this is a clearing out of old energies and patterns. In time, new ego structures will re-form. It is important to be patient and not to react nor leap into avoidant behaviour. As I well know, this process takes its own time and cannot be rushed.

My own inner crisis began in earnest after my second passionate and catalytic meeting with Lisa, which happened just outside Waterford, Southern Ireland, in June 2010. We spent a week enjoying coastal walks and each other's company. Because of the intense romance and passion, I experienced this gateway as initially light, happy, and ecstatic, before it shifted into something diametrically opposite.

After returning to the United Kingdom, my relationship with my partner Ursula was in freefall. The pressure of being in love with Lisa and the pain of separating from Ursula, who I still deeply cared for, threw me into a deep well of grief that was long and bitter. This sparked another round of what I call 'kundalini' waves of energy. I had to avoid any overstimulation, and meditation in any structured form was almost impossible. I did try mindfulness of breath and Metta Bhavana meditations at a Buddhist centre for several months, once a week for an hour, but that was about as much as I could manage.

Some forms of meditation, such as creative visualizations or shamanic journeying, seemed to make the waves more intense, so I stopped doing them. I felt vulnerable and fragile, and I could not tolerate too many external demands. I also found I needed more alone time, but if I overdid this I felt lonely and needy and desired just to be around friendly people. I moved out of the home I shared with Ursula for three months. Then Ursula and I agreed that I would come back and live separately in the spare room until we had decided what to do. I felt that we both needed time to come to terms with the separation.

This was my first experience of the 'dark night' in this transition, and it lasted for several months, which seemed like forever at the time. Lisa, in the meantime, had gone back to America in April 2011, and I thought that that was the end of that. During this time, I gave away many clothes and other possessions to different charity shops. I would often walk to the local parks, where I threw away many crystals I had collected over the years and several precious silver rune rings. I had the feeling that I needed to lighten the load for the unknown journey ahead.

By the end of 2011, I had moved out of the flat and Ursula and I had finally separated. Around the same time, I was receiving emails from Lisa that were becoming more flirtatious and romantic. (Lisa's sunny and playful personality was something I always loved about her.) At first, I responded neutrally, but eventually I thought it would be a good idea to visit her in Texas. So in January 2012, I jumped on a plane to see her. It was wonderful to see her again, and although

Texas was very different to mystical Ireland, this did not stop another round of romantic merry-go-round. We talked about marrying, and I resigned as a director of Alternatives the day after returning to the UK.

Fast-forward several weeks, and the relationship with Lisa ended dramatically and abruptly. I did not realize it at the time but she had done her job and it was time for her to move on. I quietly slipped into shock, despair, and then numbness and a terrible feeling of being alone and disconnected from the world around me.

This was my second 'dark night' experience, and although it lasted less than a month it was no less difficult. The experience was especially intense for about 10 days. The kundalini waves had returned, and I began shattering crystals around me and interfering with all manner of electrical devices. (I explained this to friends and colleagues, as house and office electrics started blowing around me and the internet became erratic, and was mostly met with incredulity.)

The kundalini experience was reactivated with a force. I had dark visions of entering a vast grey wilderness, and try as I might I could not shut these visions out. They would enter my mind, both day and night, and it felt that I was somehow locked into this bleak landscape. To add to the frustration, there seemed to be a great light in this wilderness that was far away and unreachable. Strangely, during this period, I felt drawn to churches and would sit in silence and light candles, praying for help and guidance. In time, I intuitively felt this far-off light in the wilderness to be connected to Christ consciousness, but I could not tell if the light was in any way concerned about me or not. I tried to reach out for this light in my visions, but it remained far off and seemingly disinterested in me.

My local church in Church Street, Stoke Newington, London, had a stained-glass window with an image of Christ praying and the caption, 'NOT MY WILL BUT THY WILL BE DONE.' This stained-glass window of Christ on his knees seemed to sum up my predicament. I could not force anything with my personal will, and I had no idea what the greater Universal Will wanted of me. Pray as I might, I felt nothing. My connection to my Higher Self, which had been built over 20 years of spiritual practice, felt like a hazy dream. Similarly, my intuition was blown. I felt ungrounded and disconnected from all meaning, purpose, or love. To say this was 24/7 torture is possibly an understatement. My existing life had been well and truly shattered, and the journey ahead looked far from promising.

> *Are you willing to be sponged out, erased, cancelled,*
> *made nothing? Are you willing to be made nothing?*
> *Dipped into oblivion? If not, you will never really change.*
> — *D. H. LAWRENCE*

SPIRITUAL EMERGENCE EMERGENCY

If you feel you are going through a spiritual emergence or even a spiritual emergency, then here are some useful tips to help you through:

EMOTIONAL SUPPORT — Find someone to talk to who is knowledgeable about spiritual emergence, perhaps a coach, spiritual teacher, or friend who has been through a similar experience. Avoid judgemental people. Do not share your core experiences with people who cannot understand what you are going through.

PRACTICAL SUPPORT — Stay away from emotionally disturbing images, movies, flashing bright lights, and loud music. Avoid anything too overstimulating. Avoid sexual contact for a time. Try and find silence through your day. When you feel the need, spend time with people who uplift you or who are empathic to your situation.

NUTRITIONAL SUPPORT — Be conscious of what you eat and drink. Stay away from stimulants of any kind—such as alcohol, caffeine, and sugar. Eat as much organic raw food as possible, and avoid processed foods as far as possible. Take omega oils and essential minerals. Drink as much pure water as possible.

PHYSICAL SUPPORT — Gentle exercise, such as walking or swimming, is helpful. Avoid overstimulating massage, but gentle bodywork such as reflexology and craniosacral therapy can help you stay grounded in your body. Nurturing touch and nonsexual holding-hugging is helpful.

SPIRITUAL SUPPORT — Avoid intense spiritual practices for a while, until you feel more stable in yourself. Simple prayer and lighting candles are fine and mindfulness of breath practice can be useful. Only when you feel stronger and more stable is it advisable to engage with a steady spiritual practice.

ENERGETIC SUPPORT — If you take baths, use sea salt as a way to purify your energy field. Shower regularly, and imagine white light cleansing your energy field. Use flower essences or homeopathic remedies to stabilize or handle shock or stress. Reiki or similar energy healing techniques can be helpful.

MEDICAL SUPPORT – This is a tricky one, and I would suggest that only if the situation is serious or dire, or if there is an real absence of any support systems, should hospitalization be considered. Similarly, I would suggest that psychiatric drugs should be considered as a last resort. Although they help to stabilize an individual going through severe spiritual emergency, they are not designed to support spiritual emergence.

CALL ON SACRED UNITY

- Remember that you are an integral part of the web of life. This might be difficult right now, but it is so nevertheless.
- Remember that you are part of the Unity of Creation. Call upon the All That Is to watch over you and guide you on your journey. Ask for the power of love and clarity to guide you, and ask often for clearing and healing.
- Remember that there is love around you, even if you cannot feel it right now. Even though you may you feel disconnected from love, remember that love is the most powerful force in the universe.
- Remember to feel the light of the sun upon you, the solidity of earth beneath you, and the comforting power of nature around you.

9

Song of Metamorphosis

*Sometimes, it seems to me that when you walk
down this path of finding yourself
all the other paths vanish... .
It is through this journey that we discover
the instrument we truly are.*

— *RASHEED OGUNLARU*

Recalibration is the transformational engine room of transition. In a smooth transition, the old life is shed like a snake gracefully shedding its skin. There is little pain or drama involved. Here, the vision is fixed on an enticing future that evokes expectancy, excitement, and wonder. This does not mean that there are not times of doubt, or even mild disorientation or bewilderment. Life will always throw in the random factor so that things often do not work out exactly as planned. This is no cause for concern. If the vision, desire, and drive are strong, then forward momentum continues.

Sometimes, our dreams work out better than we could have ever planned. Then again, there may be times when our drive falters and our momentum slows down. Whatever the speed of our journey, the real activity is happening deep down in the soil of our psyche. In winter, out of sight, nature is preparing for the coming spring. The same thing happens in recalibration. Our beliefs and values are shifting beyond our conscious awareness. This is the real alchemy of recalibration. When our beliefs and values shifts, so does our sense of direction and belonging in the world.

There is nothing we need to do. Our soul and biology are running the show. Here, we just need to sit back and trust the process. If we have left a painful reality, then recalibration gives us the space to reflect, rest, and recover before deciding on our next steps. Beyond the previous phase of letting go, we are now touching a new psychological space of silence and spaciousness. Eventually, we start to feel what author Deepak Chopra calls 'the field of infinite possibilities' stirring deep within.

Michael was in his early thirties. After he resigned from a stressful career in local government, he accepted an invitation to visit a friend living in Wales. 'After working in a busy office for many years, I enjoyed the sharp contrast of not having to think very much and of being able to just hang out in nature. At first, it felt almost heretical to chill out in the garden or take long walks along the coastline. But soon I felt the ocean, the rocks, trees, and sky all seemed to be enticing me towards a new life, one far away from stressful workloads and boring office politics. I only stayed a couple of weeks, but the power of that time was a powerful turning point for me.'

Sometimes, we are in a more neutral space and just need space to reflect on our next steps. Rachael resigned from her job and went to India to reflect on the next phase of her life. 'It wasn't that I disliked my job; it was just that something more was calling me. In India, I just relaxed and chilled, then I started to get really enthusiastic about a number of ideas. I would wake up in middle of the night and write. I asked myself a number of questions, such as what I liked and what I was good at. I knew people were always important, and I was interested in themes of confidence and motivation. I thought about selling these ideas as coaching and training packages to the business world. The advice I received from a business coach back in the UK was that I needed a niche. I never took that advice. I work on a combination of intuition plus hope. I knew I could not force the process. Looking back, perhaps it sounds a bit naïve, but it worked out fine. I learnt to be good with ambiguity and just play with ideas.'

Perhaps, we do not need time for rest, healing, and integration; we just want to get on with things. Clare had a vision: she wanted a child. After trying with her partner for three or four years, she was beginning to think it would not happen. Then suddenly it happened, and she felt elated. She told me there were physical challenges in the early months, and she thought she would lose the baby, but everything smoothed out.

We met when she was six and a half months pregnant, and she told me: 'In the early months of the pregnancy, I felt a whole octave shift. What it feels like to be me has shifted. It is mysterious, really, but it feels really right. Somehow, a whole piece of my neurotic patterning has been taken out. I used to be an anxious person. Now I feel I have less worries.'

After releasing some old, limited thinking patterns, Clare felt she had the space for another important project. 'In my spare time, I finished a manuscript for a children's book, and now I am waiting to get it published. I feel between the worlds in both respects. I am waiting for my baby and my book to be born into the world.'

Whether we are leaving an old life or moving more directly into a new phase, recalibration can be an alchemical space of openness, self-inquiry, and exploration. Recalibration is an opportunity to more fully enter the moment and let go of any concerns about past and future. One way to do this is to practise what is known in Zen Buddhist circles as Beginner's Mind.

RECALIBRATION AND BEGINNER'S MIND

- Accept nothing at face value; adopt a healthy scepticism;
- Let go of everything you have learnt from experts, teachers, or gurus;
- Drop the language of should, must, and have to;
- Stop, appreciate, and experience the present moment fully;
- Notice what is unusual and unique in every situation;
- Reflect on your dreams, but let go of attachment to the end result;
- Focus on the big questions and simply allow the answers to come;
- Look for one uplifting thought or idea in your conversations with others;
- Adopt a sense of newness with people you have known for a long time;
- Do something small, different, and unexpected every day;
- Take one step at a time, without worrying about the future;
- Immerse yourself in your life, and forget what is going on around you;
- Enjoy being surprised, especially when things do not work out as expected;
- Celebrate falling down as well as getting up again;
- Learn to embrace the unknown and live each day to the full;
- Practise saying 'I don't know' at least once a day.

THE INNER GARDEN (MEDITATION)

In this meditation you will be exploring an important goal or new project as pure energy. In this way, you can clear any energy blocks and expand what you think is possible by playing with light, colour, sound, and space.

Find a time when you can relax and not be disturbed. Sit or lie in an open body position, and begin to notice the in and out breath and the space in between. Remember that you are light. Your soul is light, and the universe is made up of light. As you breathe in, notice that you can invite light into your body with each breath and breathe that light into the cells of your body, for our body is usually hungry for light. With each out breath, imagine you can release any energy that does not belong to you or no longer serves you. As you breathe in, notice that you can breathe light into your bones and blood; as you keep breathing in light and releasing old energy, your body takes on so much light that a white mist forms around you. In this mist, notice a pathway.

Take a step onto this pathway, and follow it through the mist until you come to a spiral staircase leading into the heavens. Ascend this staircase, and at the top you will come to a short path that leads to a garden gate. This is the entry point to your higher conscious mind. Notice how you feel, standing here. Through this gate is a beautiful garden where you can relax, heal, and also plant seeds for the future. Step through the gate, and enter the garden. Here, the garden is still. It is winter, and there may even be a light frost on the ground. In this space, notice there is a higher light and vibration in the garden; everything here is a reflection of your inner light, your authentic self. When you step through the gate, trust your first impressions, notice the colours, sounds, and smells and sights of the many varieties of trees, plants, flowers, and wildlife here.

Here, in the garden, you can meet a new project or important goal as pure energy. Find a clear space in the garden where you can bring a project to mind, and evoke it before you as a shape and pattern of pure energy. Just trust your first impressions. Notice the size, shape, colours, and patterns of this project as energy. Know that your soul is a master artist, and you can play with energy. You can add colour or light or shape to this energy pattern before you. Make it more beautiful, radiant, and spacious. Perhaps, you can add a rainbow light to this energy field and see how it feels. Play with changing the patterns and size of the energy field. You can create more space within the patterns of the energy field and see how that feels. Play with adding sound or music to this energy field. Notice how you feel when you make these changes. Imagine you could add qualities such as joy or success to your goal or project. You can also play with stepping into this energy field and see how it feels on the inside. When you are done, allow the energy project to shrink to the size of a large diamond, and bring that diamond into your heart or third eye for safekeeping. Please know you can come back here anytime and work with this project or another as pure energy.

When you feel ready to leave the garden simply return the way you came through the gate, making sure you close the gate behind you, and back down the spiral staircase and through the white mist. Take your time to slowly return to everyday consciousness. It might be a good idea to journal about your adventures in the garden for this will help to anchor and integrate your experiences.

In the midst of difficulty lies opportunity.
— *ALBERT EINSTEIN*

Rough Recalibration

At a social gathering, a man in his early sixties described to me his experience of a rough transition. He felt he was 'going round a sharp bend that never seemed to end!' Crisis leaves us disorientated and shaken. Soul tension has sunk the ship of our old life, leaving us bereft and uncertain about what to do next. Recalibration is about finding the resolve and strength to keep moving, rolling with the punches and not forcing events, and allowing the magic of this part of the journey to do its rejuvenating work. For some, recalibration is a time to heal from a traumatic time.

When I met Gemma, she had an interesting story. Recalibration was for her an important time for healing. Gemma has been working in conflict areas for 10 years. She worked in North Uganda for a time and then went to work in Palestine after finishing a master's degree. Living there, she was faced with the reality of occupation on a daily basis. Gemma confessed: 'Eventually, I decided to come home and take time out, and I spent a month in Thailand. I was sad, lost, and confused, and it helped to some extent. Working in war zones, you are expected to be the hero without showing your emotions. I now realize that it is not helpful to bottle up my anger, grief, and sadness. Crying or being angry is not allowed. When I came back to the UK, I went for some healing and then everything erupted. I could not stop crying. I seemed to lose myself. I felt a depth of depression I had never experienced before. I would just cry at unexpected times and places. This lasted for several weeks. I went back for more treatments, and the therapist said she had never seen a reaction as extreme as mine. I just kept on going, and eventually it began to subside. Now, I do not know where my life is going, yet after this process I feel more okay with uncertainty.' On the rocks of crisis, Gemma found that she could heal her past. Recalibration can be a time of reflection and of clearing old patterns and fears. Greta was planning to marry and just could not go through with it. At the last minute, she jumped ship and returned to her native New Zealand to reflect and rethink her life. She had been adopted as a child, and she knew there were some unconscious patterns around her early childhood driving her life. After some reflection, she realized that she had always been terrified of being alone. This led her to impulsively jumping into romantic relationships.

Recalibration for Greta was about facing her deepest fear, which she did for long periods of time whilst teaching yoga at a holiday resort in Greece. This experience gave her a sense that she could make her way through the world by herself. The last time we spoke, she was getting on a plane to India. This felt even scarier than going to Greece by herself. When we spoke she was thinking of aborting her trip, but after some encouragement from me and a few other people, she got on the plane and had an amazing adventure.

Recalibration can also feel like being in a void—like the caterpillar that enters the cocoon not really knowing what will happen next. When Bea came to London in the early nineties, she was homeless for a time before finding a studio flat in south London. This was not just a home to her; it was her sanctuary. Although she had strong resistance to moving on, she eventually put the flat on the market. It took several months to sell and then she put her belongings in storage and essentially packed up her old life. She went to live on the south coast of England for some months, to get a new perspective on her next steps. She waited and reflected, but nothing much opened for her.

Then she moved to Italy and sent me this message on Facebook: 'I'm living 10 minutes' walk from the beach; the house has amazing sea views. Yet I am in the middle of a massive void, with no idea how to proceed. I am between two worlds. I don't live in England anymore, but all my stuff is there in different places…. I am in Italy with no idea on how to proceed….'

A few months later, she sent me another message: 'It's been quite a process, and the process goes deeper still. My brain at times does not function properly, and I crave constant stillness and solitude. I am the void…. I am walking on faith….'

For Bea, crisis came in the form of not feeling she belonged anywhere on the earth. I encouraged her to accept that she was nothing more than a happy wandering nomad at the moment.

NO MUD, NO LOTUS (MEDITATION)

This meditation is for when the stress of crisis begins to soften and you can relax and go within to do some energywork.

Find time when you can relax and not be disturbed. Sit or lie in an open body position and begin to notice the in and out breath and the space in between. As you breathe in, notice that you can invite light into your body with each breath, and with each out breath, imagine you can release any energy that does not belong to you or no longer serves you. Keep breathing in light and releasing old energy from your body until you notice a white mist forming around you.

Step into the mist, and keep walking until it clears and you find yourself standing before a door. Notice how you feel about this door. Describe it to yourself. On the other side of this door is a landscape that reflects your current journey. When you are ready, step through the door and close it behind you.

On the other side, you notice that you are standing in a landscape. Trust your first impressions. This landscape is a psychological reflection of your current journey. Here, look around, and you will find a path or a road. Stand on the path or road. Know that one way reflects your past and the other your future. Begin to explore the past, and notice how your mind is reflecting to you, metaphorically, your current outer world journey.

Take note of where the path is difficult or broken. Imagine that you can begin to repair the path in your mind. Make it more stable and broad. See if you can add colour and sound to this path, such as the green of nature on both sides of the path and the sound of birdsong or a gentle wind.

When you are finished, begin to explore the direction of future. Do the same here. Anywhere the path seems less stable or broken, imagine it being repaired. Again, call in colour and sound to make the path more beautiful and enticing. Perhaps add structures where you can rest and eat.

Imagine many helpers on this path, both in human form and in spirit, assisting you on your way. Go as far as you can and notice if the path splits at any point. Explore both pathways, and notice which one feels the right one for you. Perhaps one choice is a dead end or is totally blocked at a certain point. Then place a sign at the crossroads to let your conscious mind know which path is the right one to take when you meet this choice in outer reality.

When you feel ready to leave this place simply return the way you came, through the door to the path and the white mist. Take your time to slowly return to everyday consciousness. It might be a good idea to journal about your inner journey, for this will help to integrate the work you are doing here.

You might find that inside the sadness, the grief, the despair lies something else too. Lies some kind of beauty, some kind of humanity, human understanding that understands that things are impermanent that nothing stays the same. That there is loss, that it's not possible to control the whole universe.

— *JON KABAT-ZINN*

Recalibration is the fearful caterpillar in the cocoon becoming the future butterfly. Here, suffering is transformational. Melanie Reinhart, master astrologer and writer, says, 'When suffering opens the heart, many different dimensions of experience enter in and the more flexible our understanding the deeper our healing.'

One man found his 'butterfly' self in prison. He was sent there because of his political views in the winter of 1964. He was confined to a small cell, the floor was his bed, a bucket served as a toilet. He was forced to do hard daily labour, breaking rocks. He was allowed one visitor a year for 30 minutes and could write and receive one letter every six months.

The experience of Robben Island prison transformed Nelson Mandela into the wise future leader of a free South Africa, where he received over 250 international awards, including the 1993 Nobel Peace Prize. Very importantly, his time in jail gave him a deep compassion and lasting belief in the dignity and worth of human life. Nelson Mandela passed through his final transition in this world in December 2013. His courage, vision, and leadership will be long missed in this world.

RECALIBRATION: BECOME THE WITNESS

Recalibration is a great space to develop a witness consciousness. This is about developing more awareness and being a little more detached from what is happening inside and around you.

- When you wake up, spend five minutes being present to yourself by noticing the natural rhythm of your breath;
- Be mindful about eating. Notice the sensation of hunger. Take your time and savour each mouthful. Get present to the sensation of drinking. Avoid being too full. Always leave some space in your being for more;
- Get present to what you are doing. Feel the world around you. Notice colour, textures, sounds, silence, and smells, as you move through the world;
- Become more aware of the subtle shifts in mood and feelings that happen as you move through your day;
- Reduce the activities that prevent you from being present, such as watching TV, mindlessly surfing the net or playing computer games, or

unconscious retail therapy. Bring more consciousness and awareness to everything you do, both the ordinary and extraordinary;

- Be present to the way your body moves throughout the day, and notice when you feel contracted-expanded or happy-unhappy at different times and in different circumstances;
- Live by the natural rhythms of your body rather than the demands, deadlines, and dictates of the clock;
- Begin a daily meditate practice in order to create a habit of stillness.
- Make washing the dishes or bathing your body a mindfulness meditation;
- Consciously change your daily routines. For instance, change the times you eat, where you go to eat, and what you eat. Try periods of not eating and see how that feels;
- Bring your attention each day to contemplating the really important challenges in your life without racing ahead to find solutions. Just bring more consciousness and spaciousness to each issue, one at a time;
- Bring your awareness each day to contemplating the really important questions in your life, without seeking to know the answers.

And so long as you haven't experienced this—to die and
so to grow—you are only a troubled guest on the dark earth.
— JOHANN WOLFGANG VON GOETHE

Super-Rough Recalibration

A super-rough recalibration feels like a tumble from a state of grace. The inner flame of light disappears, taking with it all guiding sense of purpose and meaning. The foundations of the old self are shaken to the core, and existing ego structures crack or collapse. From personal experience, I know that words can never fully describe such an arduous passage; yet, at the same time, there are great gifts here if we can endure.

Mystical kabbalah describes this as 'crossing the abyss,' an initiation into higher consciousness that involves the dissolution of the ego or the separated self. Crossing the abyss is the spiritual journey of surrendering the dualistic ego to higher consciousness—a death and rebirth passage made doubly difficult because in the approach it seems like our Higher Self has abandoned us in our hour of need. All intuition and spiritual connection vanish like a morning mist. To understand this space, simply think of Jesus crucified on the cross crying out, 'My God, why have you forsaken me?'

Deep abandonment makes the passage all the harder to bear. Yet here, as we wander seemingly alone in the darkness, we must maintain the faith that our Higher Self is always with us. For this is the case, even if we cannot feel it. We must pass through the abyss; there is no turning back. The tarot card The Hermit (I am thinking particularly of the Aleister Crowley deck, as painted by Lady Freda Harris in the late 1930s) represents this journey perfectly. Here, an old man in a state of withdrawal and seclusion has turned away from the everyday concerns of the world. The introverted figure is bent downwards, holding aloft a lantern as he walks into the abyss. Here, diamond-like rays of light shine into the lower regions of darkness, revealing Cerberus, the three-headed dog, guarding the entrance to the underworld. This is the path where everything that is not truth is stripped away.

This process can feel brutal and challenging, because there really is not just one process; it's more like five happening all at once.

1. EGO STRUCTURES

The soul tension and resulting underworld journey has created intense psychic pressure that, in recalibration, eventually leads to a cracking or dissolution of restrictive or outdated ego structures. The old structures are giving way to the new. Problems usually come because of the speed of the process—the old structures collapse before the new ones are in place. This creates a sense of fragmentation, disorientation, and disassociation. We do not know ourselves as before, and we cannot process the world in the same way. One friend described this process as feeling like her 'psyche had exploded.' Here, we are releasing the old self in a dramatic way before generating a new sense of being in the world. In the meantime, we can feel raw and vulnerable in ways hard to describe. Rest and ease, and sometimes professional help, are essential if not always possible.

2. THE HIDDEN SHADOW

In the abyss, we encounter the archetype that Carl Jung called 'the shadow.' The shadow is everything we think we are not, or fear we are. It is what we judge most harshly in ourselves, and therefore, it is what we cast far from our consciousness. As our primary ego becomes more fragile, this allows the hidden shadow to come to the fore.

Author Denis Linn says of the shadow: 'Your shadow self is the part of you that stays unknown, unexamined, and out of the light of your conscious awareness. It is the part that is denied or suppressed because it makes you uncomfortable or afraid. Whatever doesn't fit your image of your ideal self becomes your shadow.'

We must remember that the shadow is our ally, not our enemy. The shadow contains gifts that we have thrown away. But energy cannot be destroyed so easily. Here in the shadow, we may find our repressed anger, forgotten jealousy, old disgust, fear, violence, or helplessness. Everything we exile into the shadow, we lose touch with in ourselves and project onto others. If we cannot feel our fear or violence, then others will reveal it to us. It is not only our dark traits we exile into the shadow; this is where we throw away our light. But in the underworld of a rough transition, we are dealing here with the dark shadow. (The light shadow follows in renewal, bringing back much lost potential.) Here, we can meet our old hate or rage or grief. These shadow parts seek integration, which can feel confusing and overwhelming.

3. ANCIENT KARMA

Added to this, we may also encounter old unconscious blocks and programs that are coming to the surface to be released. These can be mental/emotional imprints from this life and/or other lives. Karma is defined in the Bible as the harvest of the seeds of action we sow in life. If we sow rhubarb seeds, then we will get rhubarb, not broccoli. If we sow hatred and dissent, then this is what we will harvest. If we sow generosity and goodwill, then this is similarly what we will harvest.

In terms of other life karma, where a pattern has been created in other existences, then it may come to a head in a transition. For instance, if we have been prevented from speaking our truth in other lifetimes, then this will seem to intensify in a transition before breaking apart in recalibration and renewal. In a super-rough transition, we may encounter karma from our family or the collective—for example, we can meet violence and hatred that is not ours alone. Here, we are helping in our own way to witness and dismantle such heavy patterning. Old patterns can be revealed and also intensify during a transition, as they are being transformed in recalibration.

The fruit of this is mostly felt in renewal. If you suspect you are dealing with family karma, then Family Constellations work can be very healing. If you are dealing with other life or collective karma, then it is worth looking around for a good healer or an appropriate methodology you can learn and use yourself.

4. DISCONNECTION FROM SOURCE

To make things extra-difficult, we have to make this journey without our intuition or any help or prompting from our Higher Self. There is so much psychic movement going on that our connection to the light seems cut. This is not exactly the case, but it is often the overriding experience. Here we face existential loneliness. Writer Paul Brunton says: 'The sombre loneliness experienced during the dark night of the soul is unique. No other kind of loneliness duplicates it, either in nature or acuteness, although some may approach it. It creates the feeling of absolute rejection, of being an outcast.'

5. OUTER LIFE TURMOIL

Although the main turmoil is internal, this does not mean that there is nothing very much going on in the outer life. Change is still likely, perhaps in the home, or with friends, lovers, health, or work. All change takes a certain amount of energy to deal with, and concentration and focus are now more difficult. With everything else going on, even mundane things like paying the rent or travelling around town can seem overwhelming. Emotions may still be releasing from the previous phase. Grief will take its own good time to clear. We may feel angry, confused, or overwhelmed about what is happening. There may seem little support in the outer world. Few friends or family members may understand such a journey. To understand requires some personal experience of the descent, and because of our disconnected, superficial, materialistic, modern lifestyle, most people simply do not have this.

What is to give light must endure burning.

— *VIKTOR E. FRANKL*

The Dark Night Deepens

In recalibration, the 'dark night' can deepen. In the previous phase, the dark night is a result of resistance to the process. Here, the dark night is about deep inner transformation. This is a mythic descent that can seem frightening and distressing, to say the least. As mentioned above, in kabbalah, the journey is known as 'crossing the abyss.' Ancient cultures speak about this journey through myths, the earliest being the descent of the Sumerian Goddess Innana, who abandoned all the glories of heaven, opening 'her ear to the Great Below.' Innana made the heroic passage down through the seven gates barring the way to the underworld, surrendering her jewels and clothes along the way. Thus she was only allowed entrance when she was stripped and naked of all attachments to the upper world.

A later myth is that of the Greek goddess Persephone. Although the classic version is quite dark, in another version Persephone is said to have gone willingly to comfort the despairing cries of the dead. And in another more modern version, Persephone was the one who seduced Hades.

Later tales, such as *The Divine Comedy* by Dante, speak of the journey into Hell and Purgatory. References to the underworld and the abyss can be found in more recent literature, such as Tolkien's epic *The Lord of the Rings*, in which the wizard Gandalf leads the Fellowship of the Ring deep underground, into the Mines of Moria, where Gandalf falls from the bridge of Khazad-dûm. There, he passes through a great trial of fire and water and is later resurrected by the Elven Queen Galadriel. (On this important point, the screen version by Peter Jackson deviates from the original story.)

When I met Margaret, she told me about her dark night. 'When my dark night happened, it felt like my whole life was crashing down around me. I did not recognize myself anymore. I felt that someone had just pulled all the walls down I had built up around myself and my life. The physical and emotional pain was extreme, and I felt like I would have done anything to have the pain taken away. I just wanted to scream. I felt so much anger, sadness, depression, and hurt. This extreme level of pain lasted for two weeks before becoming more tolerable.'

Erin's dark night came after the end a relationship. She was granted some special leave from work and decided to go off backpacking for three months to clear her head. While she was away, she heard that she been let go from her job.

'I went to a café in Amsterdam and had a joint. It was all very legal, and it was something I had done many times before. However, this time was different, and I felt that over a period of four days, I slowly was building up to a manic high. I was feeling high and blissful, and then I then started to have a conversation with God. When I came back to the UK, a few days later, I felt completely paranoid. I could not sleep, and I kept looking at the shadows on the wall, which somehow convinced me that I must be in hell. I refused to leave the house (I was staying with my cousin at the time) because I feared that I was going to be taken away. Eventually, I *was* taken away—to the local psychiatric hospital. In the ambulance, I just remember screaming "Yes" and "No" all the way.'

Lisa (not to be confused with the catalyst in my own journey) went on a visit to Glastonbury with her mother, and the trip brought up lots of unexpected emotions. 'I just felt so angry, and I felt I had to leave and so I left the second morning. When I got home, I found I could not function, I felt depressed and sad for no reason. Then one day, I lay on the kitchen floor and could not get up—I just curled up in foetal position.'

This experience went on for months. She had frequent panic attacks and often thought about suicide. She started to make a will and tidy up her affairs, although happily she lived to tell the tale!

SACRED DARKNESS (MEDITATION)

Find a time when you can relax and not be disturbed. Light a candle with a clear intention for your journey, such as clarity or healing. Sit or lie in an open body position, and begin to notice the in and out breath and the space in between. As you breathe in, notice that you can invite light into your body with each breath, and with each out breath, imagine you can release any energy that does not belong to you or no longer serves you. Keep breathing in light and releasing old energy from your body until you notice a silver-grey-white mist forming around you.

Step into the mist and see a path. Follow the path, which leads to a door. When you are ready, pass through this door, which opens up to a landscape. Here, you will find somewhere a great chasm that is wide and deep. Stand on the edge of the chasm, and look down into its depths. Perhaps, you are already in the chasm; perhaps, you are about to make the descent.

Wherever you are in your journey, this is a time to pause for prayer and reflection. Look around your inner world, and find a place to rest—perhaps beside a pool of water, a rock, or a tree. When you have found the place, consider what internal qualities or practical help you need for this journey. Perhaps you need courage, guidance, or support. Perhaps you need healing or help handling overwhelming emotions. Perhaps you need help in stabilizing your ego self.

Here, pause to send a prayer to your Higher Self or Sacred Unity. Ask for protection and help with psychological overwhelm. You could imagine lighting a candle on a rock or tying a ribbon onto the branch of a tree. It is important to affirm your light, even if you can only feel darkness around you. Do not worry if you cannot feel a response. This is quite common. Just know that your Higher Self and guides are watching over you right now and protecting you from harm.

When you are ready, leave this place and return the way you came. Pass back through the door. Return to the silver-grey-white mist, and find the path that leads back to your body. Take your time to slowly return to everyday consciousness.

IMPORTANT – Do not attempt this meditation alone whilst deep into a 'dark night' experience. You can make the journey if someone else you trust holds sacred space for you. Journaling the experience of this meditation can also be useful.

This is my delight,
Thus to wait and watch at the wayside
Where shadow chases light...

— *RABINDRANATH TAGORE*

My own dark night began during the release phase, and it lasted until the end of recalibration. No words can really convey the pain of this time. My world had turned to ashes, and this feeling was beyond grief or depression. The ground I was standing on was breaking under my feet, and any sense of stability was hard to find. I had become some shuffling mechanical ghost moving through outer rituals of my life.

I remember two occasions when the pain felt particularly unbearable and I found myself gazing down at the river Thames contemplating jumping in. I stood there in silent meditation, contemplating death and the ending of this darkness. Time heals everything, and after several months, the worst of the symptoms passed and I was able to function normally in the world.

The second dark night began in March 2012, when Lisa finally left me. I felt it the moment it happened. I was lying in bed, awake—I could not sleep, which was unlike me. Then it felt as if my heart centre exploded, leaving a gaping hole behind my heart. I felt betrayed, angry, and once again adrift. There were a few angry emails from my side and some frustratingly reasonable responses from Lisa. Not long afterwards, Lisa cut off all communication, and that was that.

I sought help from a brilliant healer from America, who somehow put me back together again, working with me long distance via Skype. The pain in my heart was healed in an instant. But the healing did not prevent me from once again plunging into a dark night. This time, the experience was much darker and more intense than before. Now, there were no mere visions of barren wasteland; instead, I was confronted by dark underworld caverns and threatening entities. I could not shut out visions of large spiders, snakes, and fiery daemons blocking my way. If I tried to meditate or if I simply closed my eyes for too long, the visions would swarm over me. There were also recurring night dreams of being chased by angry mobs or by armed soldiers. I felt evermore paranoid and worried that somehow my visions and night dreams would manifest around me in the outer world.

After about a month the dark night quickly subsided, taking with it the terrible feelings of despair and meaninglessness. However, the grim visions and night dreams continued on and off for many more months. Fortunately, I was able to process these experiences and visions in therapy.

In one session, I closed my eyes and very quickly found myself in the underworld, facing a huge black spider some several feet in diameter. (I suffered from a phobia of spiders as a child and could not bear to be in the same room with the tiniest of spiders.) The spider barred my way for some time before exploding into several large green snakes with open jaws and threatening fangs.

I could not move, and as I stood there, a strange and beautiful dark-haired woman entered the cavern from a hidden door several feet away. She wore a long, flowing, white dress and had shoulder-length hair and black alien-like eyes that radiated raw power. She gracefully reclined on a bench several feet away without for a moment taking her eyes off me. I felt like I was being scanned. Then, when she seemed satisfied, she stood up and gracefully stepped forward. The snakes parted and slithered away into the darkness as she stretched out her arms towards me.

I trusted her and allowed her to take me in her arms. Her embrace was comforting, like a mother embracing her child. I remember we both grew in size, and I was transported back into the house of my early childhood. In that journey, I felt a great healing from some old wound. After this, the dark visions shifted. Instead of meeting threatening creatures, I was able to walk unchallenged through tunnels and rock-hewn halls.

The dark night was beginning to ebb towards the winter of 2012 and into the early months of 2013. In March of that year, I signed up for a Metatronic Healing course in Abingdon, just outside Oxford. It had been three years almost to the week since my romantic break in Galway in Ireland, in 2010.

During a group healing transmission, I had a powerful vision. I was walking along passageways fringed with hot, flowing, orange and orange-red lava. I came before a great granite staircase that led up to some great height. I climbed the staircase and could feel the raw solidity of stone and earth power. Below was granite and fire, and above, in the night sky, a mantle of countless stars.

Reaching the top of the staircase, I stood suspended between Heaven and Earth. As I looked up, one star caught my eye, and I watched it became brighter and pulsing with light. Then a column of silver-white liquid light poured down from the star, into my crown chakra and into my outstretched hands. I caught the light, and it seemed to flow through me, enlivening every cell of my body with its healing power.

The light poured out through my feet and base of spine into the rock below. Here, white star fire danced with orange-ruby earth fire. Somehow, this dance reflected a great healing in me, and it signified my time in the underworld as virtually over. It seemed by luck, fate, or divine intervention I had endured. I was no longer afraid. I felt free at last. The darkness had no power over me anymore. There I stood in the underworld, a glowing figure of white-and-orange fire, standing in the receding darkness.

PRACTICAL ADVICE

- Most importantly, the underworld journey cannot be forced. Time is the great healer. Avoid trying to push or force your way through;
- Here, there is nothing to fear except fear itself. Everything is a reflection of your consciousness, and nothing can harm you;
- Stay with the pain. You are cleansing old wounds, some of which might be ancestral or part of the collective, and so beyond rational explanation;
- Rest as much as you can. You are being recalibrated from the inside out. New ego structures are forming that are helping you integrate dark 'shadow' traits;
- Try simple meditation, such as mindfulness practice or the Buddhist loving- kindness meditation to still the mind and clear any anxiety;
- Do not think you have to be here on your own. Find supportive friends. Be around non-judgemental people. Go out and drink tea in beautiful places. Do things that feed your spirit. And if you haven't already done so, find a good therapist;
- Walk and sit in the wildness of nature as often as possible. Hug a tree, sit by a body of water such as a still lake, breathe out any stuck energy, ask mother earth to cleanse you;
- Release energies that may not belong to you or no longer serve you. Take regular sea salt baths. Use vibrational medicine. See a healer. Use any

technique that helps to release karmic energy from your physical and energy bodies;

- Immerse yourself in ordinary daily routines. Remember: 'ordinary and simple' are good. Set practical daily tasks to help focus your mind.

A Sweet Dawn

In the depths of winter I finally learned that
within me there lay an invincible summer.
— *A L B E R T   C A M U S*

In the dark soil of winter, we came face to face with our deepest fears and wounds. Yet, finally, we pass through 'the shadow of the valley of death' and enter renewal. Irish writer John O'Donohue wrote that it is 'the paradox of spiritual growth that through such bleak winter journeys we eventually come through a hidden door into a bright field of springtime that we could never have discovered otherwise.'

This so perfectly describes the process. In renewal, we recover after a difficult passage. We still need rest and healing, but the way is now open and there is lightness, hope, and steady liberation.

Maya went through a super-rough transition where everything fell away—her marriage, business, and some close friends. She went through her own mini 'dark night,' which involved considerable grief and anxiety. In renewal, she found a new life opening that included a new home near the sea and new work. She told me that on the one hand she had never felt so free, and on the other, she was still learning to trust that the ground was not going to open up and swallow her whole.

Renewal brings a growing sense of trust and grace. Most of the inner work has been done by now. The dark night fades, and a new dawn begins to illuminate our lives. We met Jasmine earlier in the book. After meeting a catalyst who threw her into a 'dark night,' she passed through a dark winter and is now in the early light of spring.

I asked her about what she had learnt: 'I wanted to know the light of another, instead of finding my own. I wanted someone else to tell me I was okay. Now, I experience the peace that comes from knowing I am okay. My life now feels qualitatively different. I am more in a giving space than taking. I am not coming so much from lack; I am now coming more from love. I decided to stay and work through all the issues in my marriage. This was the right decision for me. Now I find pleasure in all the simple things in life.'

We met Tanya earlier on, when she had a diving accident that led to her old life falling away. I met up with her when she had stepped more fully into the spring phase of her transition.

Tanya told me: 'After the accident, everything fell away—study, work, friends, my interest in sport—and I was left wondering who I am. On the other side of this difficult transition, I began to feel a new identity form, one that was interested in spirituality and alternative forms of healing. Now, everything is different: my values, the way I am in the world, how I see the world, my friends, interests, and the work I feel drawn to.'

Renewal in a super-rough transition can bring gifts of spiritual awakening or deepening. I met Loan at a friend's book launch, and we began chatting and agreed to meet again over tea. At the time, I had no idea Loan had been through a recent transition. We started to chat, and I soon discovered Loan had had a kundalini experience in 2010 whilst at a summer festival. It began during a massage. The masseur touched some points on her back and, suddenly, energy flowed up her spine and she jolted and screamed loudly. Later, during a trance dance, energy started to uncontrollably move up and down her spine in waves.

Her journey through this experience included physical pain, crying and freaking out, increased sensitivity, shaking, head feeling like it was going to explode, and greater need for periods of aloneness.

She told me: 'Now the experience has mostly passed, it feels surreal. I feel incredible consciousness and love now, where I didn't before. I get in a space of love without attachment; it is a place I can access quickly, a blissful place where I am in touch with myself, where I do not react. I feel everything I need to know is within me; I do not need to look externally. Looking back, I realize I wanted a change of direction and I couldn't achieve it, and so this experience came to assist me. I am just at the beginning of a complete redesign of my life.'

I would say that there are no good and bad transitions; there are just different degrees of challenge, movement, and transformation. Sometimes, a transition is not a new dawn in this world but a transition to the next.

I lost a dear mentor and teacher, Gill Edwards, at the end of 2011. I had trained with her for nearly nine years. She woke me up from a deep sleep in 3-D reality. Her death was something of a shock, to say the least. She was very public about her own personal transition, which she wrote about in her last two published books, *Wild Love* and *Conscious Medicine*. Just before her passing, she wrote this public letter:

I'm so sorry that some of you may be feeling grief and loss. I think the loss of someone we love is perhaps the hardest challenge that anyone ever has to face, so my heart goes out to you. What I can say is that we can make the experience far worse, or far better, by the way we see it. As I understand it, pain always means that we are not seeing things as our higher self sees them… . If you have been touched by my death, then my understanding is that you and I had a contract to part around this time, for all the gifts that it would eventually bring to you—which you will only understand when you look back in years to come. You may have done some workshops with me, and I'm sure you know (in theory) that death is not a tragedy; it is simply the choice to make a transition from one state of consciousness to another. Yes, it would be easier if I had chosen just to retire and no longer respond to emails—but somehow you have to come to terms with the choice I made. For whatever reasons, this lifetime was finished for me.

I am still very much here, but just not embodied any more. Love is an eternal bond, and you only need to think of me with love and I will be there, connecting with you. But you will only be able to sense me when you release the grief, and simply connect with the love… . You might be amazed at how rapidly you can find peace again, once you get your energy flowing and reconnect with your higher self (who sees nothing as bad or wrong).

You can focus on what is wrong or missing—my death—or you can choose to focus on what is positive. I have gone physically, but I am absolutely fine and you are still here—and so many good times lie in store for you still, with many other people to love and be loved by. If you look for what is positive in life, and things to be grateful for in each day, and choose to think only of happy memories of me, you will begin to release the grief—and then you will begin to attract more positive events

and opportunities in your life. Focus on what you enjoy, who you enjoy being with, and what dreams you have for the future. It might take time, but you can do it. In the meantime, there are hundreds of comforting books about the afterlife which show

beyond any doubt that life is eternal, and that the only reality is Love. I wish you all the very best with your journey. It will get easier—and so many gifts lie ahead.

With love and blessings,
Gill Edwards

I still very much miss the wise, intelligent, pioneering, loving presence of Gill in this world. I witnessed her help awaken so many. Her public letter is a clear reminder that death is not a transition to be feared; rather, it is one we must prepare for. Whether a transition is in this world or the next, the renewal phase is like the sun dawning on a new day after a bleak night. The dawn brings with it a sense of hope, magic, and wonder. There has been a great clearing, and the old vibrations of chaos, depression, and despair are displaced by a higher vibration of growing stability, inner peace, and slow joy.

We met Sita in Chapter Four. She had experienced a kundalini awakening that led to a period of great emotional instability, and much of her old life had fallen away. I asked her about her experience and she told me: 'This was not a gentle process, but on the other side I feel purified. It is as if the fire of the experience burned out all my old impurities. My worldview has completely changed. I have much healthier boundaries now than before. I feel more grounded in the world. I have a lovely home and a new sense of purpose.'

I asked Sita what advice she would give to anyone going through a similar process and she replied: 'For me, acceptance of what is happening made all the difference. This was not easy but necessary. So my advice is to just let it happen and then the experience becomes a lot easier.'

In renewal, we feel the call to adventure and feel the impetus to explore what is meaningful and important in our lives. Spiritual teacher Adyashanti says of this time: 'To the extent that the fire of truth wipes out all fixated points of view, it wipes out inner contradictions as well, and we begin to move in a whole different way. The way is the flow that comes from a place of non-contradiction—not from good and bad.'

In recalibration, we met the shadow and began to integrate disowned abilities and qualities. This is not always a fully conscious process, and much happens in the dream state. The lantern of the hermit has revealed much that was hidden. In renewal, we realize, hopefully, that the 'shadow' is our friend. Much like the recycle bin on a computer, it saves stuff we want deleted, but fortunately, our light and dark traits are not deleted only hidden. Here, deep in the psyche, are stored forbidden aspects of the self that were mostly jettisoned as we were growing up. A transition helps return these shadow aspects, ending an internal war of suppression that, in turn, frees up much psychic energy for renewal.

I entered renewal in the first few months of 2013. I had managed to process my feelings of anger and betrayal and had come to realize that Lisa the catalyst was a 'soul friend' and not a soul partner. I had faced the 'dark night' and processed some deep ancient terrors. I had survived and was feeling more open and hopeful. I had met 'shadow' parts in dreams and visions that seemed to contain great violence and hate. I had also met a dark goddess in the underworld who had helped me clear fear and heal a deep painful childhood wound. This was all aided by being in long-term therapy, which can be immensely useful in a super-rough transition.

My fragile ego structures were healing, and in the early summer of 2013, I visited the Rodopi mountain range in Southern Bulgaria, a hauntingly beautiful and mysterious wooded region largely populated by wild bears, cats, and wolves. Rodopi, according to legend, was the home of the mythical singer, musician, and poet Orpheus, who journeyed into the underworld to find his deceased wife.

Whilst in the Rodopi region, I took a hike with a small group at the crack of dawn to a nearby mountain sacred to the Thracians. Fortunately, there were no wild animals around (at least none we could see) as we climbed the mountain in twilight. At the top, we waited silently and breathlessly, as the sun began to rise slowly over the distant mountainous horizon. Light spread across the landscape, and time stood still. To me, this blissful and magical moment was a perfect metaphor for the dawning of a new phase of life.

SIGNS OF RENEWAL

The signs are:
- An easing and then complete release of inner darkness;
- A fading of pain, fear, and confusion;
- A growing sense of inner stillness and spaciousness;
- A return of the light of the Higher Self in daily life;
- A growing sense of aliveness and optimism;
- A rebooting of our guiding intuition and inner knowing;
- A deeper connection to our authenticity and wisdom;
- A renewed sense of belonging on and to the earth;
- An emerging clarity of purpose and direction.

Hardships often prepare ordinary people
For an extraordinary destiny.

— *C.S. LEWIS*

Renewal After a Rough Winter

A rough transition brings us through crisis to the hope and light of renewal. When Susie was diagnosed with breast cancer she was advised to have a mastectomy and chemotherapy. She decided against this, and instead explored other alternatives such as diet and lifestyle changes. After several months she got the all-clear.

'I knew it would be all clear. Now I feel I have been given a second chance. On the other side of this journey, I think I am softer, open, and vulnerable. I can live life at a different pace and do things that I would not normally do. I have started to go singing and dancing. I just want to explore stuff.'

Susie told me she wants to start living from the centre of her life, rather than just waiting for life to come to her. She started to dance, sing in a choir, go to weekly hot yoga, and she even came on a writing retreat I was running in Greece in the summer of 2013 and we had a wonderful time together.

We met Paul earlier in the book. Nine months after his partner's death, he fell through a roof and severely damaged his back. In hospital, he had lots of time to reflect on his options, his priorities, and the way he wanted to work and earn money in the future. I met Paul on the other side of his transition, when he had a new loving partner and was retraining for a new line of work. The transition, difficult though it was, had weaved its magic and moved him to a happier phase of life.

Simon, the 'Artful Dodger,' had a turning point whilst burgling a house, followed by another in prison. Whilst in jail, he thought about some of the deeper issues of his life. He told me that he was sharing a cell with someone who could be called a hardened criminal by the age of 18. He felt that jail was the bottom point of his life.

'I just sat there and asked the question, *What drives me?* The only thing that came to mind was a feeling that I could be more. I did not realize it at the time, but jail was a kind of death for me. I saw from this point on that I had a choice. It was then that I made the choice to step away from that world of crime.'

Simon's transition was about embracing fear and dishonesty. He really wanted to know his authentic self. After jail, he went into acting and quite soon had an amazing break.

'This felt better than any drug I had ever taken. My senses were heightened, and for long periods I felt I was in an altered state of consciousness. I found a deep appreciation and gratitude for the magnificence of life being birthed in me. In time, I moved away from acting and started a media company, and here I began a new adventure, exploring transparent communication. I am now writing a book on my experiences. I truly could not have imagined from that prison cell all that time ago that I would be doing what I am doing now.'

Simon is a wonderful example of someone who hit rock bottom and came up singing and dancing.

We met Bea in the previous chapter. When she entered the early stages of her renewal, she told me: 'I feel like I am still in transition… . A new beginning is happening, though at times it is still up and down. I am still working on being okay with moving and not having a fixed place to live and settle. I am still in Italy, staying in a house with great sea views. I cycle around all the time, exploring the coastline. Last night, I swam in the sea at sunset, then stayed on the beach 'til very dark, sitting in stillness, looking at the stars… .'

In the winter of 2013, she rented an apartment by the sea on the east coast of Italy. Just before Christmas she sent me this message. 'Sitting in my lovely study, I have sorted the desk and have placed my laptop on it ready to write. I have wonderful sunsets over the hills from this room.'

By early 2014, she was more settled in another house by the sea and sounded more happy and stable. I feel happy she is finding a real sense of belonging in the world at last.

I had not seen Sonia for some years when I bumped into her at a festival, just after finishing this book. She asked me what I was doing since leaving my previous job, and I told her about my ideas on transitions.

As she listened she started to smile, and intrigued I asked her if she has been through a transition herself. She replied: 'Sure, for the last four or five years. It was full on, but now I feel all that suffering was somehow worth it. Life now has completely opened up and I just feel such an ongoing sense of fullness and grace.'

A RETURN TO FLOW

Mihaly Csíkszentmihályi (the author of *Flow*) identified a number of factors that generate the experience of flow:

- There is a clear goal that is attainable with one's skill set and abilities. The challenge level and skill level are both high. There is a balance between ability level and challenge. The activity is neither too easy nor too difficult;

- There is a high level of concentration on a limited field of attention. The activity generates a tremendous focus. There is a loss of self-conscious-ness and a merging of action and awareness. There is a distorted sense of time where the subjective experience is altered;
- There is a sense of personal control over the situation or activity;
- The activity is intrinsically rewarding, which leads to an effortlessness of action;
- There is an absorption into the activity, narrowing the focus of awareness down to the activity itself. There is a lack of awareness of bodily needs, to the extent that one can feel hunger or fatigue without realizing it;
- There is a direct and immediate feedback, so that success and failure in the activity becomes apparent. This allows for action to be adjusted as necessary.

To live is so startling it leaves little time for anything else.
— *EMILY DICKINSON*

Renewal After a Smooth Winter

Renewal is well described by Beat novelist and poet Jack Kerouac in his line, 'I saw that my life was a vast glowing empty page and I could do anything I wanted.' It can be hard to distinguish between recalibration and renewal after a smooth transition because, relatively speaking, the journey has not been that difficult. Renewal brings a gradual sense of stability and certainty after a time of rapid change. As we step towards our dreams, there can come a growing sense of confidence and possibility as doors start to open.

Two good friends of mine, Damo and Katrina, met at a dinner party in my home, and soon they were romantically involved and living together. Not long afterwards, Damo was offered a job in America, and they both decided to go and have an adventure living in Malibu, up in the canyons with a great sea view for a year. During this time, Damo proposed to Katrina, and they got married on an idyllic Greek island in the summer of 2010.

They had a dream to return to the UK, to live by the sea, but before returning they decided to visit Katrina's parents in New Zealand and Damien's parents in Australia. Damo had a property he was selling in Melbourne, and there were chal-lenges and delays in selling the house. Finally, it happened, and they found a perfect building on the South Coast of England to create a home, yoga studio, and organic cafe. The project was to prove physically, emotionally, and financially demanding.

After a challenging 18 months, I visited them in their completed home. I asked Damo what he had learnt as a result of the journey.

'I was always a fiercely independent spirit, and I had to learn—both in my marriage and in the building project—to co-create with others. The journey has deepened my trust in life and opened my intuition and creativity. I have been stripped naked of my old life and left totally curious and vulnerable to the new.'

I put the same question to Katrina and she replied: 'This journey gave me the opportunity to be myself, to heal my past, and to co-create something magical with someone I love and adore. We passed through a financial void by trusting our intuition. The right people just kept showing up to help us.'

A smooth transition can change the way we approach the world of work and also change our experience of time. From my point of view, Damo and Katrina seemed to swap places psychologically and energetically after the transition. When I met Damo, he was a hard-working Internet entrepreneur. When I first met Katrina, she was doing some temping work for the National Health Service and feeling lost in her life. Now, Katrina is on track in her yoga business, and Damo has slowed down to a mellower pace of life, exploring creativity through photography.

Erica was in a respected corporate job, earning lots of money, and yet she wanted something else. She started listening to self-help and spiritual talks, and they confirmed what she had to do.

'I took a leap of faith and resigned from my corporate job. I followed up on an offer from a friend to work on a family farm in Ireland. It was beautiful and I discovered that by stripping away the noise of the city I could connect more easily with my inner self. It was here that I started writing. Now I am back in England I want to continue writing. Now I have connected with my inner self, I know my experience is not location dependent. I can connect within anywhere. I just needed that strong reference point of space and silence. Now I am much more trusting of the whole process.'

Deep inside the earth,
Unknown seeds are praying
Creating new life,
Already kissing
The dawn of spring.
— *DEJA HU*

The Activation of Dormant Gifts

The term 'self-actualization' comes from the work of the theorist Kurt Goldstein, who believed realizing one's full potential, meaning 'to express and activate all the capacities of the organism,' is a basic drive in the human psyche. In a smooth transition, a form of self-actualization happens as a result of following through on an important goal or project. In a rough transition, we self-actualize or awaken as a result of navigating external challenges. In a super-rough transition, we navigate internal challenges that can awaken our dormant inner light. Whichever path we tread, much will be revealed about ourselves and our hidden abilities, gifts, and talents that was previously hidden. This is an organic process that keeps on building the further we go.

Satish went on an 8,000-mile pilgrimage, visiting the graves of Gandhi in India and John F. Kennedy in America, and also sought to deliver a humble packet of 'peace tea' to the then leaders of the world's four nuclear powers. He walked over the Himalayas to London, via Paris and Moscow, and he crossed the Atlantic by boat. The journey took him two and a half years. He carried no money and depended on the kindness of strangers. I chatted with him and asked if he ever went hungry or could not find shelter. He told me that when there was no hospitality on offer, then 'this was an opportunity to fast and sleep under the million stars hotel!' He made this heroic journey to highlight the need for a world without guns.

He went on to found a holistic college and became a long-serving editor of an ecological magazine. For many years, he taught workshops on ecology and holistic education and became a much-sought-after speaker on these subjects. His inner teacher has long been active in the world.

One friend of mine went through a super-rough transition that involved a period of great emotional instability. We met whilst she was very much still processing her journey. She told me that her creative juices really sparked at the point her journey seemed darkest. Then she began exploring journaling to help with her general well-being and also other mediums that allowed her creativity to flourish. It seemed quite evident to me that her inner artist was being activated.

THE ACTIVATION OF DORMANT GIFTS

Renewal witnesses the release of new gifts, qualities, and abilities in the psyche. These are held within certain archetypal energies that can be thought of as seeds hidden deep in the soil of the psyche. These are mostly dormant within us until usually a transition process awakens them, then they begin to stir into life and start to blossom in renewal.

ARTIST — This seed contains your untapped creativity, innovation, spontaneity, play, and fun. The world needs more artists. Begin to explore art and creativity in all its many forms until you find the right form for your creative essence to blossom.

AWAKENER — This seed contains your ability to act as a catalyst for radical change. The world is waking up now and needs your awakening. Explore opening to a higher vibration of light in your energy fields. Explore transmitting energy through your words to create change. Your powerful connection to Sacred Unity will touch and inspire others.

DREAMER — This is an ancient seed that has largely been forgotten for thousands of years. This seed contains your feminine potential to dream your reality into being. The world needs more dreamers right now. When this seed becomes active in your life, then you can use it to dream Heaven on Earth.

GUARDIAN — This seed contains your ability to care for the kingdoms of nature. The mineral, plant, and animal kingdoms are suffering right now in this global transition. This seed can also awaken as a guardian of the light in young, incoming souls. Begin to explore your potential for nurturing and protecting the light in all other life forms.

HEALER — This seed contains your potential for healing. Healing can happen in many forms and guises. Healing does not always require a formal setting. There are many hidden healers in the world. Why not begin to explore healing with a smile, hug, a loving thought, or a kind gesture. This seed will enable you to heal people as well as the mineral, plant, and animal kingdoms.

HERO — This seed opens you to greater levels of courage, determination, faith, and perseverance in your daily life. Transition involves risks and requires courage. It is essentially a hero's journey, which is why this seed is most commonly activated. Discover the hero you were born to be.

INNOVATOR – This seed holds your inner genius. A transition can restructure the way you think and see the world. You are here to nurture and follow your inner genius. Do not worry if others see you as eccentric; you are meant to be different and to follow your own path. Try things out; experiment and network with others who inspire you!

LEADER – This seed holds your unique leadership potential. Ancient Celtic kings and queens knew that to lead was an act of service. You serve as a leader. The leader awakens qualities such as strength, inspiration, and power—the kind that serve the life force rather than dominate others. You are here to be visible, shine, and serve.

LOVER – This seed contains your ability to give and receive love. The lover follows a tantric path, whether formally or in their own way. The lover explores the full potential of vulnerability, fun, play, and gentleness. Work with sensuality and the polarities of sexual energy to enthuse and enliven your life.

MAGICIAN– This seed holds your ability to create and co-create reality with the greater intelligence in the universe. Why not begin to explore your qualities of imagination, intention, and focus. (This seed is connected to the dreamer, but it is relatively more yang, or active in the world). As a magician, you are here to work with energy, vibration, and the power of the spoken word.

SAGE – This seed contains your ability to see the unity of all life. The sage understands the illusion of separation, and in this fire they are reborn. Often, this seed is activated in certain people when they become elders. You are here to share your spiritual wisdom, whether through words or your silence.

SYNERGY – This seed contains both masculine and feminine qualities. The divine feminine knows itself through love, holding sacred space, and relating. The divine masculine seeks to know itself through focus, purpose, and action. When the two aspects of self unite, we experience synergy. When the two forces unite within you, then you become the expression of divine unity and balance.

TEACHER – This seed contains your unique ability to coach, mentor, and teach. This may be in a conventional or non-conventional sense. Your skill is in transforming complexity into simplicity. Be ever curious, and follow your desire for knowledge and wisdom. You are here to open, uplift, and inform others.

When patterns are broken, new worlds emerge.
— *TULI KUPFERBERG*

Going Deeper Into Renewal

In renewal, I began studying astrology, something I had put off for years because I simply did not have the time. These studies helped me to connect some of the dots of my journey. What follows next is for those of you with some basic knowledge of astrology.

My Chiron Return came in 2007. (My natal Chiron is in Aquarius, the 3rd house, and this transit slowly activated my inner writer, leading to two books written and published between 2011 and 2014.) Saturn, with its demands for greater efficiency, simplicity, and realism, entered my sun sign of Libra in October 2009. Saturn passed into my chart ruler of Scorpio in October 2012, where it will continue to grind its way through until September 2015. Saturn transited my Scorpio ascendant in mid-December 2013, which is said to herald a new phase of life. As if all of this were not enough, two other astrological alignments were on the horizon. First, a Grand Cardinal Cross in April 2014, with Uranus opposing my natal sun, Pluto and Jupiter squaring it, and Mars conjunct. Then the all-important matter of my approaching second Saturn Return in 2015! So all of this points to 'change central,' as one astrologer put it.

In renewal, psychological and spiritual shifts can continue for some time. In a smooth transition, it is more a case of adjusting and opening to the new. In a rough or super-rough transition, it is about healing and stabilizing, as well as opening. In the beginning months of my journey into renewal, I would wake in the mornings as if I have been working physically hard all night. Also, as I discovered, renewal is not about immunity from difficult feelings. I still had moments of feeling afraid, anxious, angry, hopeless, and disappointed for some months before it cleared completely.

Now, being further in, I feel older but wiser. I know I have more psychological and spiritual tools at my disposal. In my own journey, I found more time on my hands. I happily spent more time in silence and aloneness. I have also become even more intuitive and sensitive to energy, I feel people and places more intensely, which is not always easy. Because of this, a daily practice of clearing out lower vibrations and connecting with the higher light has been important. I would often imagine light spinning in my energy fields, and I would call on angels and guides to clear out lower astral sticky energies. Walking in nature has always been helpful, along with body practices such as yoga and Pilates. As mentioned before, the physical body can often feel the intense strain of a transition and needs rest and recuperation.

Renewal after a rough or super-rough transition is not a time to sit on our laurels and wait for the next miracle to come along. There are still challenges. In July 2013, I nearly drowned while swimming in rough seas in Greece. This incident was a knock-on effect from another incident in January of the same year, when I helped put out a house fire. In the process, I breathed in black, toxic fumes. Despite being given oxygen by fire fighters afterwards, and being checked out by my GP, a week or so later I discovered all was not fine while I was out in a rough sea. This was a close call and a strong reminder of the final transition that awaits us all. It was also an interesting metaphor for my own super-rough transition.

Now, in early 2014, the kundalini experience that was triggered in 2010 seems to have settled down. Before then I had to take great care not to do anything too emotionally or energetically overstimulating. Now, *Insha'Allah* (God willing), as the Muslims say, I no longer feel the volatility of the process, and instead feel more steady.

I am now living in a small yet lively spiritual community in Bethnal Green, East London, which continues to feel like a sanctuary and a home. Here, I have found friendship, laughter, and belonging. My grandchildren, Eva and Isabella, born during my transition, continue to grow and blossom. My time with them often feels akin to going through an army assault course of love!

I remain on happy terms with my ex-partner Ursula. One evening I asked her if she had any regrets, and she replied that she had 'never felt happier,' which was truly consoling to hear. Ursula is now pursuing her wish to be a healer, using the vehicle of a system called Life Alignment. (I have had many healing sessions with her, and I know she is truly gifted.) She is in a stable and loving relationship and very happy. She said something to me one day that remains with me. 'You never have to stop loving people, just because you are not living with them.' I find this thought very helpful and heart-warming.

Ursula's son, Ian, whom I co-parented between the ages of four and 14, is now a mature adolescent living with his father in a community in North London. He is finishing his A' levels and contemplating university and life.

Lisa, the catalyst who sparked the adventure, is still very much in touch. Lisa has gone through her own transition, and now she is pursuing her life mission as a teacher and guardian of bright young souls in the world. She has been regularly updating me on Facebook, and in a message in the summer of 2013, spoke about her unfolding life. 'My creative projects are showing life… . This year is looking even better … . I am so grateful to be doing this work.'

Shortly afterwards, she was offered a leadership role in an organization working with pre-school children. Rather poetically, she commented: 'I feel the big opportunities ahead as well as the responsibilities and challenges. They're pulling me out of my cracked pot now. Fingers crossed my roots can bare the new soil!'

Leaving my work with Alternatives in December 2012 was a huge shift, and I had no idea what I would be doing in the world afterwards. In my hour of need, synchronicity kicked in and two consultancy projects emerged. These helped me to develop new skills and gave me the time to focus more of my energy on teaching writing workshops and retreats and coaching/mentoring authors. Towards the autumn of 2013 the consultancy work ended, and I scaled down the writing mentoring and coaching, and eventually stopped working altogether for about five months. This allowed me to finish this book.

At this point, several people commented on how different I looked. They said I was more carefree and younger, somehow. I took this to be a good sign. My old drive and ambition were being replaced by a larger psychological space of ease and grace. I was losing all anxiety about how it all would work out. My values were shifting. Family, friends, laughter, and joy in the moment have become more important, as has the need to dive deeply into my own spiritual practice.

In the early stages of my transition, I started to see a transpersonal counsellor on a weekly basis. This process continues to be grounding, compassionate, and insightful. Now, instead of dark dreams, I have neutral or healing dreams. There are times when I awake in pure bliss and gratitude, as if every cell of my body is vibrating at a new frequency of light.

I feel a growing alchemy, and I know, rather than just believe, that I am a co-creator with creation. I know from personal experience that Heaven and Hell are states of consciousness. I can feel into the great paradoxes of life—those of mortality versus eternity and unity versus uniqueness. I have become more politically and socially vocal on social media. Now, it is time to bring a new note of consciousness and sanity to the darkness on the planet.

In the spring of 2014, several 'doors' unexpectedly opened simultaneously. Through one door, new work entered; through another, a contract was agreed and signed to birth this book, *Personal Transitions*.

Through yet another door entered the sensual muse, and a new love connection began. (My new lover had been through her own powerful transition, triggered the same year as my own. She was just emerging into the early stages of renewal.) On our first date, walking hand in hand down the busy and colourful Brighton Lanes one Saturday afternoon, an old propeller plane did a loop-the-loop high above us in the clear blue sky, painting a gigantic heart with the smoke from the fuselage. We looked on in happy amazement and agreed that this was a good sign.

Here, in renewal, the jigsaw pieces of my life are slowly yet surely coming together in perfect timing. More adventures are ahead, no doubt. I will have much more to say in the coming years. Time, of course, will tell!

Don't cry because it's over.
Smile because it happened.
— DR. SEUSS

RENEWAL: FINAL PARTING ADVICE

- Life is about constant change and movement. Nothing remains the same forever. In renewal, life will continue to surprise you. Do not try to control or plan where it will take you; use your discernment, which helps you know when to act and when to chill and flow;
- Speak your truth. No-one is superior or inferior to another. Everyone has an equal life here. We are all part of one planetary community and equally deserve abundance, well-being, and peace of mind;
- Integrity means paying attention to your dreams, following your highest values, honouring your challenges, and having a healthy sense of self-care;
- Honour your choices. Take your time over important decisions. Move through the world with 'less haste, more speed,' as they say;
- Forgive and release the past, but do not forget it. Life is full of learning and lessons. Release baggage but not your knowledge or skills. Every skill, learning, and wisdom gained could prove useful at some point further down the line;
- Know your boundaries and limits and also your fullness, gifts, and talents. Nurture your vulnerability and your strength. Also honour the same in others;
- Follow your intuition. Act with integrity. Do what you need to do. Act in accordance with your highest values;

- Continue to process your beliefs and unresolved emotions. Do not be deterred or influenced by the limiting judgements, opinions, or projections of others;
- Follow the rhythms of nature. Rise and retire with the sun, and live simply.
- Meditate every day. Connect with the light of the rising sun, and connect to the light in the earth. Before you go to sleep, you can call on your guides and angels to be with you as you explore the dreamworlds;
- Open your heart to love. Seek out love in the world, and treat all life as sacred. We are not separate from life, so love and care for all life. As you love and care for life, you love and care for yourself;
- Having a spiritual practice and community can be so very helpful. Making peace with loved ones and family is important. Acceptance and fullness is always a better way to journey than with bitterness and regret;
- Seek out your soul tribe, those people who support your light and higher purpose in the world;
- Seek out wisdom in the world; there are many guides and teachers to be found in every corner of the earthly plane. When you are ready, the guide or teacher will appear. 'Ask, and it is given.' 'Seek, and you shall find';
- Trust that your life's journey, no matter what has happened or what is happening, is unfolding perfectly;
- Death is but our final transition from the earthly plane into a new dimension of adventure. The real question is not so much *when* but *how* we will make this transition;
- Since you are still here on the earthly plane, reading this book, I think it is safe to say that your mission here is not quite finished yet. So I leave you with this final prayer: May your unfolding journey through life be ever fruitful and ever blessed.

Bright Blessings
Steve Ahnael Nobel
April 2014

Resources

BOOKS

A Little Death – Ona Kiser (Heptarchia, 2012)

Broken Open – Elisabeth Lesser (Rider, 2004)

Callings – Gregg Levoy (Crown, 1997)

Care of the Soul – Thomas Moore (Piatkus, 1996)

Conscious Capitalism – John Mackey and Rajendra Sisodia (Harvard Business, 2013)

Conscious Medicine – Gill Edwards (Piatkus, 2010)

Crossing the Unknown Sea – David Whyte (Penguin Putnam, 2001)

Cutting the Ties That Bind – Phyllis Krystal (Sri Sathya Sai Towers Pvt Ltd., 1999)

Daring Greatly – Brene Brown (Portfolio Penguin, 2013)

Dark Nights of the Soul – Thomas Moore (Piatkus, Revised 2012)

Embracing Our Selves – Hal and Sidra Stone (Nataraj Publishing, 1988)

Emergence – Barbara Marx Hubbard (Hampton Roads, 2012)

Feel the Fear and Do It Anyway –Susan Jeffers (Vermillion, 2007, 20-year anniversary)

Flow – Mihaly Csikszentmihalyi (Rider, 2002)

Full Catastrophe Living – Jon Kabat-Zinn,(Piatkus, Revised 2013)

Identity and the Life Cycle – Erik Erikson (WW Norton, 1994)

In Case of Spiritual Emergency – Catherine Lucas (Findhorn, 2011)

Illusions – Richard Bach (Arrow, 2001)

Inward Revolution – Krishnamurti (Shambhala, 2006)

Iron John – Robert Bly (Rider, 2001)

Kundalini – Gopi Krishna (South Asia Books, 1993)

Kundalini Rising – Various authors (Sounds True, 2009)

Left to Tell – Immaculee Ilibagiza (Hay House, 2007)

Life of Pi – Yann Martel, (Canongate Books, 2003)

Living Beautifully – Pema Chodron (Shambhala, Reprint 2013)

Living Magically – Gill Edwards (Piatkus, Reprint 2009)

Living with Joy – Sanaya Roman (HJ Kramer, Revised 2011)

Love's Hidden Symmetry – Bert Hellinger (Zeig, Tucker & Theisen, 1998)

No Destination – Satish Kumar (Green Book, 2000)

On Death and Dying – Elisabeth Kubler-Ross (Routledge, 2008, 40th Ann.)

Original Blessings – Matthew Fox (Bear and Co., 1987)

Man's Search for Meaning – Victor Frankl (Pocket Books, 1997)

Prayers of the Cosmos – Neil Douglas-Klotz (HarperOne, 2009)

Rites and Symbols of Initiation – Mircea Eliade and Willard Trask (Harper Torchbooks, 1965)

Sacred Economics – Charles Eisenstein (Evolver, 2011)

Sectioned: A Life Interrupted – John O'Donoghue (John Murray, 2009)

Seth Speaks – Jane Roberts (Amber-Allen, Reprint 1994)

Soul Retrieval – Sandra Ingerman (HarperOne, 2006)

Spiral Dynamics – Don Beck and Chris Cowan (Wiley-Blackwell, 2005)

Spiritual Emergency – Stan Grof (Jeremy P. Tarcher, 1989)

Spiritual Growth – Sanaya Roman (HJ Kramer, 1992)

Sufi – Deja Hu (CreateSpace Independent Publishing Platform, 2012)

The Artist's Way – Julia Cameron (Jeremy P. Tarcher/Putnam, 2002)

The Hero with a Thousand Faces – Joseph Campbell (University of Princeton Press, 1972)

The Hero's Journey – Joseph Campbell (New World Library, Reprint 2003)

The Hidden Gospel – Neil Douglas-Klotz (Quest, 2001)

The Lord of the Rings – J.R.R. Tolkein (Allen and Unwin, 1954)

The Myth of the Eternal Return – Mircea Eliade (Bollingen, Reprint 1971)

The Nature of Personal Reality – Jane Roberts (Bantam, 1982)

The Path of Less Resistance – Robert Fritz (Ballantine, 1989)

The Road Less Travelled – M. Scott Peck (Touchstone, 2003)

The Second Half of Your Life – Jill Shaw Ruddock (Vermillion, 2011)

The Science Delusion – Rupert Sheldrake (Coronet, 2012)

The Shaman and Ayahuasca – Various authors (Divine Arts, 2011)

The Soul's Code – James Hillman (Bantam, 1997)

The Three Marriages – David Whyte (Riverhead, 2010)

The Top 5 Regrets of the Dying – Bonnie Ware (Hay House, 2012)

The Way of the Shaman – Michael Harner (Harper San Francisco, 1992)

The Way of Transitions – William Bridges (Da Capo Press, 2001)

Thirst – Mary Oliver (Bloodaxe, 2007)

Transitions – William Bridges (Da Capo, Reprint 2004)

Understanding Aleister Crowley's Thoth Tarot – Lon Milo DuQuette (Weiser Books, 2003)

Voyager Tarot – James Wanless (Merrill-West, Reprint 1984)

When Things Fall Apart – Pema Chodron (Element, 2005)

Wild Love – Gill Edwards (Piatkus, 2009)
Worldbridger – Juliet and Jiva Carter (Sowelu, 2007)
You Can Heal Your Life – Louise Hay (Hay House, 1984)

FILMS

Avatar – Film, Director James Cameron, 2009
Baraka – Documentary, Director Ron Fricke, 1982
DMT: The Spirit Molecule – Documentary, Director Mitch Schultze, 2010
Home – Documentary, Director Yann Arthus-Bertrand, 2010
Inner Worlds, Outer Worlds – Documentary, Daniel Schmidt, 2012
Life of Pi - Film, Director Ang Lee, 2013
Occupy Love – Documentary, Director Velcrow Ripper, 2012
Ram Dass, Fierce Grace – Documentary, Director Mickey Lemle, 2001
Spring, Summer, Autumn, Winter, and Spring – Film, Director Song Min-Young, 2004
Star Wars – Film, Director George Lucas, 1977
The Dhamma Brothers – Documentary, Director Andrew Kukura, 2007
The Living Matrix: The New Science of Healing – Documentary, Director Greg Becker, 2010
The Matrix – Film, Directors Andy Wachowski and Lana Wachowski, 1999
Joseph Campbell and The Power of Myth – TV, series of interviews with Joseph Campbell by Bill Moyers, 1988
The Shift – Documentary featuring Wayne Dyer, Director Michael Goorjian, 2009
The Wizard of Oz – Film, Directors Norman Taurog, King Vidor, Victor Fleming, Mervyn LeRoy, George Cukor, 1939
Whale Rider – Film, Director Niki Caro, 2004
What the Bleep Do We Know? – Documentary, Directors William Arntz, Mark Vicente, and Betsy Chasse, 2004

About Steve Nobel

Steve Ahnael Nobel is a personal and business coach and NLP master practitioner. He has many years' experience as a group facilitator, consultant, and writing mentor. For 13 years, Steve was a co-director of Alternatives, a not-for-profit organization based in St. James Church, London, which promotes self-help and spiritual author events. Between January 2000 and December 2012, Steve helped organize over 1300 author events for Alternatives.

Steve is the author of four published non-fiction books. Steve now leads writing workshops and retreats around the United Kingdom and Europe. He is also a certified British Fencing Coach (Level 1). For more information, please visit *www.stevenobel.com* (main website), *www.transitions101.net* (blog), Steve Ahnael Nobel personal page on Facebook, and the Facebook Group Transitions 101. You can follow Steve on Twitter at *London_Has_Soul*.

FINDHORN PRESS

Life-Changing Books

Consult our catalogue online

(with secure order facility) on

www.findhornpress.com

For information on the Findhorn Foundation:

www.findhorn.org